£16.99

Audit

Mental Health.

CLINICAL AUDIT IN
MENTAL HEALTH

JR   to Fay, Luke and Hannah

DM   to my dear wife Karen for all your support, and our young son Harrison for all your entertaining distractions

CLINICAL AUDIT IN MENTAL HEALTH

Towards a Multidisciplinary Approach

John Riordan
Central Psychology Service,
Thorpe Combe Hospital,
Walthamstow, UK

and

Darren Mockler
Neuropsychology Department,
King's College Hospital,
London, UK

JOHN WILEY & SONS

Chichester • New York • Weinheim • Brisbane • Singapore • Toronto

Copyright © 1997 John Wiley & Sons Ltd,
Baffins Lane, Chichester,
West Sussex PO19 1UD, England

National   01243 779777
International (+44) 1243 779777
e-mail (for orders and customer service enquiries): cs-books@wiley.co.uk.
Visit our Home Page on http://www.wiley.co.uk
or http://www.wiley.com

Other Wiley Editorial Offices

John Wiley & Sons, Inc., 605 Third Avenue,
New York, NY 10158-0012, USA

VCH Verlagsgesellschaft mbH, Pappelallee 3,
D-69469 Weinheim, Germany

Jacaranda Wiley Ltd, 33 Park Road, Milton,
Queensland 4064, Australia

John Wiley & Sons (Asia) Pte Ltd, 2 Clementi Loop #02-01,
Jin Xing Distripark, Singapore 0512

John Wiley & Sons (Canada) Ltd, 22 Worcester Road,
Rexdale, Ontario M9W 1L1, Canada

Library of Congress Cataloging-in-Publication Data

Riordan, John.
    Clinical audit in mental health : towards a multidisciplinary
approach / John Riordan, Darren Mockler.
        p. cm.
    Includes bibliographical references and index.
    ISBN 0 471 96332 1 (alk. paper)
    1. Mental health services—Evaluation. 2. Mental health services—
Great Britain—Evaluation. 3. Medical audit. 4. Medical audit—
Great Britain. I. Mockler, Darren. II. Title.
    [DNLM: 1. Mental Health Services—standards. 2. Medical Audit.
WM 30 R585c   1997]
RA790.5.R56   1997
362.2'2'094—dc21
DNLM/DLC
for Library of Congress   96-48521
                                                                        CIP

British Library Cataloguing in Publication Data

A catalogue record for this book is available from the British Library

ISBN 0-471-96332-1

Typeset in 11/13pt Palatino by Mayhew Typesetting, Rhayader, Powys
Printed and bound in Great Britain by Bookcraft (Bath) Ltd, Midsomer Norton, Somerset

This book is printed on acid-free paper responsibly manufactured from sustainable forestation,
for which at least two trees are planted for each one used for paper production.

CONTENTS

ACKNOWLEDGEMENTS

We would like to thank Malcolm Scott, former Care Group Manager for Mental Health at Claybury Hospital, for his support of the initial project and its extensions; Dr Rhupen Brahma, Consultant Psychiatrist, for his encouragement and constructive criticism; Colum Clinton, Senior Audit Facilitator, for his many contributions to the work; Maria Garcia and John Lewis, CPA Co-ordinators, for their parts in CPA implementation and data collection; the staff of Juniper unit at Claybury Hospital; Paul Clifford and Paul Lelliott for their helpful comments; and Jackie Healy and Valerie Leahy for all their secretarial skill and patience in preparing the manuscript.

Chapter 1

AUDIT: AN INTRODUCTION

Audit is the systematic examination of the efficacy of routine clinical practice. It addresses itself to the gap between what has been shown to be efficacious and/or high quality and what is actually practised in health services. Perhaps its distinguishing aspect relative to other types of evaluative activity is that it tests "ordinary" practice rather than that which is "exceptional" and associated with projects, innovations, new initiatives, clinical trials and controlled research. Audit has a central place within the new dynamic in the National Health Service (NHS) to create even stronger pressures to identify and eradicate poor performance.

To date mental health audit has been largely a series of predominantly local and apparently random studies with very different methodologies and intentions (Maynard 1993, Thomson et al 1996). The idiosyncratic nature of audit has recently prompted greater strategic co-ordination both professionally through the royal colleges and administratively through the Department of Health and the National Health Service Management Executive (NHSME). A more strategic view would place audit in a well-defined position as part of a wider cycle of quality management (Hearnshaw et al 1994) or as an aspect of evaluative activity under the banner of "clinical effectiveness" (NHSME 1993b, National Health Service Executive (NHSE) 1994c, 1995a). Audit led by the predilections and particular interests of local clinicians is being redressed by an increasing number of "stakeholders". There has been a new interest and financial control by purchasers as well as pressure by both managers and users to be allowed into the audit process.

Claims that doctors have always tried to evaluate the service they provide and treatments they prescribe may well be made with the intention of keeping audit within the professional fold (Klein 1995). Crombie et al (1993) state that the Hippocratic Oath itself was a quality statement and it has been argued that recent activity around medical audit is no great departure but rather part of a long and professionally led development with the medical royal colleges well placed to take a lead in national audit programmes (Glover 1990a, Gath 1991, Marriott & Lelliott 1994).

However, audit and quality initiatives in the NHS have been "sporadic, local and disaster driven" (Ellis 1988) or at least tending to the piecemeal and unsystematic and certainly not linked to the kind of licensing or accreditation and inspecting system of its American counterparts (Dickens 1994). Within the field of mental health for example, the British Committee of Inquiry System has existed to service "spectacular" failures and to make recommendations that might remedy problems which had fallen into the public domain (Ritchie et al 1994, Davies et al 1995, Blom-Cooper et al 1995). Similarly, the Health Advisory Service was originally established to monitor services at least once every 10 years because of a series of "scandals" in long-stay institutions (Baker 1976).

The self-evaluative tradition in medicine therefore cannot be viewed alone as being the engine for recent developments in audit although the rejuvenation of this tradition may have been one of its effects. Prior to 1989, and despite notable exceptions such as the Confidential Enquiry into Maternal Deaths (Godber 1975) and the similar study of perioperative deaths (Campling et al 1993), medical and clinical audit was limited to enthusiasts (Shaw 1989, Edwards 1991) and was not a widespread activity. The stimulus to audit came largely from the 1989 government White Paper, *Working for Patients*, and in particular the addendum *Working Paper 6* (Department of Health 1989a), which clearly spelt out the government's intentions to make the auditing of medical care a linchpin of its market-orientated reforms with the effect of pushing it rapidly and successfully up the agenda for the new trusts and purchasing authorities and for the professions themselves (Glover 1990a).

Medical/clinical audit is part of the much wider agenda of change and reform which was introduced into the health service by the government in the early 1990s. These reforms can be viewed as aimed at increasing the flexibility and efficiency of the system, thereby enhancing the quality of health care, or as the redesign of health care delivery system along lines that would make it more able to cope in a time of overall fiscal constraint. Either way the fundamental means for accomplishing these goals was by the creation of market-like competition for purchasing and providing various health services. With public-funded services which could not be subjected to the full rigours of the market a policy close to continuous evaluation was substituted ("the evaluative state"). Klein (1995) notes a similar aspect of policies as being driven increasingly by the "productivity imperative". However, there is also the more laudable argument which arises from medical ethics, namely that efficiency in health care is not just desirable but an ethical impera-tive since wasting resources means losing the opportunity to provide beneficial treatment to someone else (Williams 1988).

UNIVERSAL PRESSURES

Health care reform was one of the international epidemics of the 1990s (Hurst 1992), with almost all countries emphasising improve-ment of efficiency. Twin pressures seem to be simultaneously affecting most health systems across the Western world (Wyke 1995), namely dramatic cost-cutting aimed not just at reducing costs alone but also stopping the totals from spiralling: and the emergence of "patient power" as evidenced by increasing dissatisfaction with health services, and resistance to poor quality and attempts at rationing services. In the UK context, for example, £42 billion was spent on health care in 1992, a figure amounting to 6.7% of trend gross domestic product (GDP) (OECD 1995) whilst at the same time the public perception was that the standards of service within the health system were actually falling.

Lessons from abroad have also been to the forefront. In the USA a perennial "health care crisis" (Swinehart & Green 1995) arose from the fact that more of that country's gross national product (GNP) was being spent on health care than any other nation, with a vol-uminous increase in both new doctors and hospital beds resulting in something like a 40% oversupply of such beds across the country; with national systems of state-sponsored health insurance schemes (Medicare and Medicaid) undergoing a burgeoning of costs as a result of an ageing population and the growth of private health care employee insurance schemes. Much of the health resources in

America had been spent at the diagnostic and investigative end of medicine. Even today 70% of all doctors are specialists and only 30% general practitioners, a situation which is a mirror image of our own (Weiner 1994).

The "out-of-control" nature of US health spending was taken as a salutary lesson in the necessities of reform and has resulted in recent times in the whole-scale shifting of decisions away from physicians to managers and other organisations such as health maintenance associations. Although fine phrases have been coined to justify the huge reshuffling of assets and moves to the effective rationing of care that has occurred ("disease management", "therapy management", "patient management", "managed care") all centre ultimately on the issue of cost-effectiveness. For example, in an effort to optimise benefits for patients who might otherwise incur high costs some "managed care organisations" have interposed non-clinical case managers between doctor and patient (Rodwin 1995, Bachrach 1996).

By international standards Britain is a low spender on health care (Organization for European Cooperation and Development (OECD) 1987). Expenditure in the mid-1980s was at 6% of GDP – significantly lower than France (at 9%) or Germany (8%) let alone the USA at 13% (Swinehart & Green 1995). Pincus (1996) puts the percentage of GNP spent in the USA at between 10% and 20%.

Although the UK total spending compares reasonably favourably with that of other advanced industrial economies, the UK ratio had increased by nearly 1 percentage point of GDP in five years (OECD 1995), a rate above the European community and OECD averages. Strong fiscal pressures therefore existed and do exist on health expenditure and the UK reforms have demanded renewed diligence in targeting and clearly impacting on health care objectives and improvements in service quality.

IMPACT OF THE HEALTH SERVICE REFORMS

Working for Patients, the White Paper of 1989, envisaged district health authorities (DHAs) and general practitioner (GP) fund-holders commissioning health services from provider hospital and community services, most of which became self-governing NHS trusts within a five-year period. These proposals were followed almost immediately in 1989 by a second White Paper, *Caring for People*, which set up parallel proposals for the commissioning of individual packages of care and assigned lead community care responsibilities to local authority social service departments (Welsh 1994). In a follow-up White Paper *The Health of the Nation* (1992), the government presented its health strategy and objectives. It set targets in selected areas and stressed the importance of prevention in achieving them (Jenkins 1994), the emphasis on prevention being itself a radical departure from previous Conservative thought (Lefanu 1994).

These goals were to be reflected in the NHS strategies for purchasing health care in other health-related services at the regional and district level. Upfront investments were made in computerisation, financial management, and a not inconsiderable amount spent for medical and then clinical audit as part of a pump-priming investment aimed at maintaining and improving the NHS's efficiency record. However, the outcomes of the NHS reforms in general are still unknown both generally (Robinson & Le Grand 1994) and with regard to psychiatry (Welsh 1994, Ward 1994). The move certainly reversed the trend towards greater integration of psychiatry in general hospital settings as many psychiatric services became part of specialist mental health or community trusts. Particular worries were expressed about the vulnerability of outpatient psychodynamic psychotherapy where treatment may be costly and outcomes difficult to quantify (Ward 1994). The reforms have given impetus to cost-effectiveness, evaluation and innovation in the development of new and briefer psychological therapies (Welsh 1994).

It has been suggested that the "quality" initiative owed more to the changes brought about by the Griffiths Report of 1983 than to those introduced in 1991 (Klein 1995), often on a Total Quality Management (TQM) framework drawing heavily on standard setting and the work of Donabedian (1980) on structure, process and outcome. Although these developments were historic by the time of the split into purchaser and provider the introduction of "contracting" implied that the quality of services was no longer assumed to be a matter strictly for the professions. Doctors had for the most part been unaffected by the 1984 introduction of general management which produced many positions as directors of quality assurance at district level for old district nursing officers, and these posts gradually introduced a greater concentration on "quality" aspects of care at least for nursing and other professions who were in the general management line. However, medical care was largely unaffected and Cape (1995) argues that medical audit was designed, at least in part, to fill this gap.

CONTRACTS

The move from trust to contract has meant that the quality of services in the NHS is no longer taken for granted. According to Klein (1995) the reforms marked the transition from an organisation based on trust to one based on contract and were inevitably threatening to those working in the NHS insofar as they represented a switch of emphasis from autonomy to accountability. Purchasers increasingly specify quality requirements in their contracts with providers: accreditation systems have been introduced to test the organisational capacity of providers to deliver services to an adequate standard (Brooks 1994). The definition of quality used in contracts has to date often been limited, concentrating on such matters as waiting times, discharge dates and response times rather than requiring specific standards in the delivery of clinical services. However, as time has gone on purchasers have had access to much better advice, both written form and from consultancy.

Performance indicators and standard setting and monitoring are important elements in any quality assurance scheme (Dickens 1994) and have an important part to play in any system that involves audit, inspection or accreditation of providers. Accreditation and licensure are seen as essential elements of quality assurance in user services by some authors and the USA and Canada have the most well-developed systems. In Britain creditation is usually limited to the accreditation of individual practitioners through their professional bodies. The Kings Fund Organisational Audit Programme set up in 1989, described by Brooks (1992), took the North American accreditation organisations as its model. However, such accreditation systems are not without their drawbacks (Ovretveit 1992). There are doubts concerning their cost-effectiveness and the difficulties imposed by a proliferation of bodies each with different standards, as is the case in the USA, and research showing little difference between those institutions that were accredited and those that were not.

MEDICAL/CLINICAL AND MULTIDISCIPLINARY AUDIT

Within this cascade of reform, medical/clinical audit has from the beginning taken a salient position. The serious intentions of the government with regard to the auditing of medical care in the UK became apparent with the large sums of money it was willing to spend promoting it. Between 1989 and 1994 £220 million was spent directly on audit projects and initiatives. By far the greater part of this went to the auditing of medical practices within the hospital and primary care sectors (£160.8 million and £42.2 million respectively). A smaller but significant sum of approximately £17.7 million was aimed at kick-starting audit in the nursing and therapy professions (Willmot et al 1995). The major resource was quite narrowly focused initially on specifically medical audit and little guidance was given on how the money should be spent – an approach described by Maynard (1993) as "letting a thousand flowers bloom".

Part of the politics around audit for the medical professions was to be successful in controlling the process and in preventing it from becoming a tool of management (Glover 1990a, Klein 1995). Medical practitioners were not tardy in their response to the guidance on audit and the funding that was allocated to facilitate it (Kerrison et al 1994). However, the audit which developed was in the main limited to consultants and their juniors and was criticised for methodological reasons (Johnson 1992); for insularity and poor integration with other health service quality and research initiatives (Stott 1993); for being simplistic and unstructured (Ovretveit 1992) and for expenditure on information systems which were not then used as sources for audit (Walshe 1994).

Because of these and similar criticisms, medical audit has been refashioned into the more inclusive concept of clinical audit (involving all members of the health care team) and addressing all aspects of health care. However, the broadening of medical to clinical audit merely implies that the audit of the work of all the clinicians involved in care should be attempted. Multidisciplinary audit is a slightly different concept as perhaps it refers to the impact of the whole team, not just a set of individuals (on the assumption that the impact of a team may be more than just a sum of its parts). It is because of this that so much guidance has been produced in recent years by the Department of Health on how these teams should actually work.

CLINICAL/MULTIPROFESSIONAL AUDIT

In 1993–4 £3.2 million was provided to pump prime multiprofessional or clinical audit (Hobbs 1994). In the financial year 1994–5 the mechanism for audit funding changed from a system of top slicing to integration with mainstream funding. It was clearly the case that the Department of Health viewed clinical audit as being key to the marketing and contracting of health care.

In its circular *Clinical Audit* the Department of Health (1993b) spelt out the fundamental principles of clinical audit: i.e. that it should

- be professionally led
- be seen as educational
- be part of routine clinical practice
- be based on the setting of standards
- generate results that can be used to improve outcome of quality of care
- involve management in both the process and outcome of audit
- be confidential at individual patient/clinician level
- be informed by the views of patients/clients.

In the UK the problems that audit was introduced to tackle were significant if not American in scale. Clinical practice varies hugely amongst practitioners, hospitals and regions and the variations remain enormous, even when allowance is made for age, sex and other variables. Where data about effectiveness does exist clinicians may ignore it for years, preferring to continue (usually indefensibly) to do what they have always done. For example, Song et al (1993) describe a meta-analysis of trials of tricyclic antidepressant drugs compared to selective serotonin reuptake inhibitors. Even though little gain in effectiveness or reduction in side effects was shown between these two drugs, many doctors continue to prescribe fluoxetine, which costs over £1 a day, despite the fact that amitriptyline costs only 9p a day.

The history of medicine is littered with treatments that "went out of fashion" (Marriott & Lelliott 1994) and the discarding of discredited interventions continues today. Drug-induced deep sleep therapy, LSD prescribing, insulin coma therapy, leucotomy (psychosurgery), electro convulsive therapy (ECT) for conditions other than depression and use of benzodiazepines in anxiety states are all examples from psychiatry. Furthermore, practice variations in extant treatments have been shown to vary widely between countries, regions and between clinicians working in different systems of health care (McPherson 1989). Marriott & Lelliott (1994) give two examples of practice variation in psychiatry: Pippard's (1992b) finding that the rate of prescription of ECT in two neighbouring English regions varied 12-fold between the greatest user and the least; and Cunnane's (1994) study showing wide variations in drug management of disturbed behaviour.

The "corrective" model to these problems might be summarised most starkly as the setting of best practice guidelines or standards by the professions and the interrogating of their peers by audit committees, identifying deviants and ensuring clinicians behave efficiently in the future. The "educational" road, on the other hand, stresses peer review, information dissemination, post-qualification development, quality improvement models of various sorts and, most importantly, the adoption and local ownership of established clinical practice guidelines.

Somewhat neglected, however, are the "psychological" resistances and processes involved in such change. The processes of behavioural change which are required to reform professional practice are not well understood. We know that evidence about effectiveness that does exist is often ignored. Information, incentives, audit and purchaser pressure to change behaviour are of unknown effectiveness and, like audit, require evaluation. The royal colleges have no satisfactory ways of enforcing audit and the possibility of disciplinary action or sanctions is anathema to most clinicians and managers. Punitive consequences stemming from audit are seen as inappropriate (Crombie et al 1993, Firth-Cozens 1993, Patten 1991) and the confidentiality of the audit session viewed as sacrosanct.

Some have doubted the wisdom of the audit investment (which is twice the annual research and development budget of the department). Maynard (1993) argues that cost-effectiveness is based on analysis of both cost and outcomes, and since for most treatments both costs and outcomes are unknown it is difficult to see on what basis audit can be grounded. Klein (1995) argues that medical audit turned out to be an example of the medical profession's ability to modify if not subvert government intentions. Consultants displayed only a fitful and erratic interest in audit despite generous financial subsidies (Kerrison et al 1993). Webb & Harvey (1994) found that their health authority's investment in an audit infrastructure and an organisation framework for audit had produced almost no benefits in the two years it was running between 1990 and 1992.

Dickens concludes that clinical audit may have a place within a quality assurance system as one element in the evaluation and monitoring of professional activity, but it does not on its own form an adequate quality control technique. Harmen & Martin (1992) describe how clinicians see audit as a matter of professional development, education and research, while managers see it as a measure of accountability for the resources used and efficiency and effectiveness. Dickens (1994) suggests the answer to these misunderstandings is the incorporation of clinical audit as one element of a comprehensive quality assurance programme that includes other methods and measures for the examination of non-clinical and managerial activity.

There has been some investigation (instigated by the NHSE) of how the large sums of money allocated to audit (approximately £350 million since 1989; Cape 1995) have been spent and with what evidence of success. The National Audit Office embarked on an investigation of the position of clinical audit in 1994 and the Department of Health commissioned "Clinical Accountability Service Planning and Research" (CASPE) to evaluate the development, progress and impact of audit in English hospital and community health services up to 1994 (i.e., prior to the adoption of "clinical audit"). The results are equivocal (Buttery et al 1993, 1995, Rumsey et al 1993). However, some feel that the £50 million spent each year on clinical audit is starting to achieve its objectives (Marriott & Lelliott 1994, Walshe & Coles 1993, Grimshaw & Russell 1993, National Audit Office 1994).

THE AUDIT CYCLE AND STANDARD SETTING

Audit is still a rather contentious issue, in keeping with its early stage of development in the UK. Although much is made of audit as a new departure there are also worries that the "infant" may never grow up. The literature is replete with models, flow charts and cookbook approaches (e.g. Marinker 1990, De Dombal 1994, Robinson 1991). Considerable confusion exists because people use clinical audit, medical audit and quality assurance to describe the same activities (Dickens 1994). It is not even clear how medical and clinical audit differ as the same definition from *Working Paper 6* is often used to describe them both.

However, "pure" audit might be understood to consist of two elements: namely, the audit cycle and professional leadership of the process. Most discussions of clinical audit return to what Russell & Wilson (1992) describe as the audit cycle (set the standard, observe practice, compare with the standard, implement change). The "audit cycle" has become almost canonical and is placed at the centre of most texts on the subject (e.g. Crombie et al 1993, Firth-Cozens 1993, Cape 1995) as the "gold standard" (Johnson 1992). Within psychiatry early work suggests a consensus that the process of audit should follow the audit cycle (Mitchell & Fowkes 1985), and that the most important part is "closing the audit loop". "Two consecutive loops" are seen as being technically sufficient (Firth-Cozens 1993).

Professional leadership likewise has been regarded as essential for audit to proceed. Early texts on mental health audit such as Firth-Cozens (1993) emphasised the local peer approach to audit, the importance of confidentiality, its educational aspects and its connection to continued professional development. The subject matter or "topics" were left to the particular interests and predilections of local clinicians. Confidentiality demanded that the raw data from a completed audit should be for the eyes of professionals alone, with aggregated data (the means and percentages) and an accompanying report becoming the "public face" of audit for a multidisciplinary team or professional group. Anonymity, not just for patients but for professionals, was felt to be essential. Aggregated results might be made available to the chair of an audit committee or to an appropriate service manager. At a higher level there should also be a unit audit report describing the activities of all the audit committees in a unit or trust.

However, a strict adherence either to professional exclusivity or to the mechanism of the audit cycle may be somewhat constraining. It is questionable whether standard setting/audit cycle is the prerequisite of audit many have suggested. Before the advent of audit perhaps the best example of a parallel clinical assessment was the "confidential enquiry into perioperative deaths" (Campling et al 1993). This followed a similar confidential inquiry into maternal deaths in 1952 and a confidential inquiry into stillbirth and deaths in infancy. Each involved a fact-finding review of all deaths within its purview and each was analysed by independent specialists. Some startling shortfalls of care, all amenable to correction, were identified. However, these inquiries were not "audit" by current standards. There were no standards set and no measure of activity against predetermined standards. The need for change was "self-evident" Hobbs (1994) and very gradual (Devlin 1996). Hobbs (1994) asks what has been established by the new approach and whether anything as clinically relevant as the National Confidential Enquiry into Perioperative Deaths (NCEPOD) reports has yet been produced.

Perhaps the nearest parallel in mental health is the Confidential Inquiry into Homicides and Suicides (Steering Committee, Confidential Inquiry into Homicides and Suicides (CIHS) 1995), which first reported in 1995, and took the view that the inquiry should continue over "many years". It may be that the standard-setting/audit cycle approach is certainly not an adequate model for describing the complexities of behaviour change in clinical practice; unless, that is, the cycle is viewed as taking place over a long period of time. Perhaps this is not an inherent fault in the model but of people's typically short-term expectations of it, the small "topic"-

based nature of much of the early audit work and a rather mechanistic view of the cycle itself.

Similarly, the problems with change and the slow pace of closing the loop (Gilles 1996) suggest the need for more involvement from managers, purchasers and others – not less – and some otherwise exemplary studies such as Pippard (1992b) can be criticised for not having involved managers more in the whole process (Shaw 1996). Perhaps in the early years, the concentration on standard-setting, topic-based audit activity and audit cycles was oversimplistic, as its local and single profession-dominated nature took insufficient account of the need for a properly co-ordinated organisational response in order for change to have any chance of occurring.

In some ways audit is a process even simpler than the audit cycle suggests. In most of the different models on offer there are at least three common elements, namely: what is good? where are we now? and how can we get to what is good? Standards set up possibilities for the contractual specification of service quality (Ashbaugh 1990) and they are also a way of translating policies into action. Standards will be derived from legal requirements, government directives, local policies and procedures. Other standards may and should come from professional good practice, research and statements of values and philosophies. The standards set, whatever they are called, need to conform to a number of criteria (behavioural, measurable, understandable, justifiable, realistic). They should be like behavioural objectives; i.e., who will do what, to what level, in what situation (Dickens 1994).

A complementary approach is outcome audit (Robinson 1991). Here the emphasis is placed on defining and measuring criteria of outcomes such as patient satisfaction or quality-of-life indicators. This is the most sophisticated and varied type of clinical audit but it has difficulties. Patients have to be followed up after discharge; measurement tools need to provide good response rates. A comprehensive approach according to Robinson is to base audit on "intermediate outcomes" which can be determined at, or soon after, discharge.

Cape (1995) believes that there are three current trends in the evolution in clinical audit. Perhaps the most influential to the future direction of audit is the recent change in how audit is funded with the increasing involvement of purchasers inevitably shifting the focus of clinical audit towards service development. The purpose of clinical audit has been to equip individual professionals and small health care teams to identify their weaknesses and improve their practice (audit for professional development) but purchasers may wish it to be designed to improve services to groups of patients (audit for service development). Secondly there is the agenda around "clinical effectiveness' (NHSME 1993b) in which a shift in investment is advocated, away from ineffective and less effective interventions and towards interventions which have been shown to be more effective (NHSE 1995a). Therefore clinical audit and out-comes studies should be used to influence changes in services, to judge the effectiveness of services and to inform patients about effectiveness related to their treatment. Finally, there is the need to recognise the views of patients and consumers and the opportunities that exist for user involvement at various stages in the planning and implementation of audit studies.

Marriott & Lelliott (1994) draw similar conclusions and speak of four related factors which will stimulate future developments in audit: namely the development of "clinical practice guidelines", greater questioning of the health care appropriateness, concern about vari-ations in clinical practice; rising consumerism and the continuing need to contain the cost of health care. We will return to some of these themes in Chapter 9.

Chapter 2

DEFINING CLINICAL AUDIT

Definition 1

Medical audit

> "is the systematic, critical analysis of the quality of medical care, including the procedures used for diagnosis and treatment, the use of resources and the resulting outcome and quality of life of the patients". (Department of Health, *Working Paper 6*, 1989)

Definition 2

Clinical audit

> "is the systematic process of setting standards for good clinical practice, comparing a sample of current practice with these standards, identifying areas which might be improved and then implementing appropriate change". (NHSE, 1996)

The medical audit definition (1, above) was published in *Working Paper 6*. It has been very influential in the early years of audit and has guided medical attempts to develop audit initiatives. The clinical audit definition (2, above) was taken from *An Audit Pack for Monitoring the Care Programme Approach* (Department of Health 1996). These definitions of audit separated by six years reflect a switch in emphasis, the re-conceptualisation of audit from one profession (medical) to many professions (clinical). The clinical audit definition reflects the developing influence of the "audit cycle" which emphasises the process of standard setting. The introduction of medical audit (Department of Health 1989a) and then the move to the need for clinical audit (Department of Health 1993b) was thought to be a move from unidisciplinary audit (mainly medical audit) to a more multidisciplinary/professional form of audit. However, it is questionable whether this has actually happened. Clinical audit would appear to be serving a similar purpose to medical audit (i.e. a uni-disciplinary activity) in that funding has been provided to professionals from multidisciplinary backgrounds to audit their own particular professional practices. Clinical audit has not led in general to a consideration of the totality of multidisciplinary provision of services and its consequent impact on outcome.

THE RELATIONSHIP BETWEEN QUALITY AND CLINICAL AUDIT

Audit is often thought of as a component of quality assurance (QA) (Marriott & Lelliott 1994) or Total Quality Management (TQM; Koch 1991). Numerous definitions of TQM have been proposed (Peters, 1987; Oakland 1989; Dale et al 1990, Dale & Plunkett 1991, Dotchin & Oakland 1992). QA/TQM is a management philosophy that advocates the organisation-wide implementation of both tools and techniques of quality control and frameworks of QA (Dickens 1994). Clinical audit was defined as one element of professional quality distinguishable from other forms of QA (Ovretveit 1991). Approaches to QA within health services have been criticised for concentrating solely on clinical audit as a means of improving performance (Berwick 1992). Berwick indicated that improvement cannot be achieved using audit alone and that an overall system of improvement needs to be implemented. The QUARTZ system has been proposed as such a model in mental health (Clifford et al 1989). The QUARTZ system identifies the principles underlying good and comprehensive QA programmes and the practical stages associated with the introduction of the programme. The following is a description of the practical stages for using the system.

FIVE STAGES TO PRACTICALLY INTRODUCING THE QUARTZ SYSTEM

1. *Commitment to service principles and a quality review strategy by service management:* Gaining the support of senior clinicians and managers, ensuring their commitment to the QA programme prior to its introduction.

2. *Selection and training of quality reviewers:* Identification of a quality review team. The team should consist of six to eight multidisciplinary senior staff acting as quality review consultants to various care areas.
3. *Quality review of setting by review consultant in collaboration with staff:* The quality review team evaluates selected care settings using the QUARTZ schedules. The schedules assess environmental resources (staffing, finance and physical environment), external links (community, agency, professional support and relationships with management), working practices (policies, procedures, teamwork and users' lives) and service provision (utilisation, programme, individual care and users' views).
4. *Goal setting and action plan by staff and submission of quality report:* Using information gained from the quality review, service deficiencies are identified and action planned involving the quality review team and the staff.
5. *Monitoring of achievement and further review in a cycle plus:* Review of the staff's progress in carrying out the action plan and achievement of goals.

To develop TQM and QA within health care services there is a need to produce mechanisms for clinical audit, the collection and feed-back of information from service users, good service user/customer care, staff training, communication and resource management (Koch 1991).

FACTORS DETERMINING QUALITY OF CARE

It is important to utilise audit and other QA methods to evaluate aspects of quality of care provision to guide service development and clinical practice. However, this raises the question of what factors determine quality of care. A large amount of information has been published addressing this question (Myers 1969, Donabedian 1982, 1988, Vuori 1982, Maxwell 1984, Shaw 1986, Ovretveit 1991, Pfeffer 1992).

Donabedian's tripartite division remains very influential within health services QA. He suggested that the quality of health care can be examined under three headings (Donabedian 1988), namely: *structure* (the attributes of the setting in which care is provided – physical environment, equipment, staff numbers, skill level, infor-mation); *process* (what is actually carried out in giving and receiving care – assessments, treatments, procedures, reviews); and *outcome* (the effects of health care on the health status of the patients).

Another influential structure for quality in health care is Robert Maxwell's (1984) six-dimensional model. His suggested headings for quality include: *relevance to need* (is the service responsive to the needs of the population it serves?); *equity* (are services provided to the local population irrespective of age, race, and socio-economic status?); *access to services* (the ease of access to services for the population served); *social acceptability* (does the service meet customer requirements?), *effectiveness* (the provision of good clinical outcome, cost-effectively, acceptable to patients and referrers?); *efficiency and economy* (increases therapeutic activity for the same costs or maintains throughput at a lower cost). The model was developed to provide objective structured evidence of quality care provision. Maxwell indicated that each of the six dimensions needed to be addressed independently, as each required different measures and assessment skills. The model was further developed using the same basic components and providing more detail (Shaw 1986).

The Joint Commission on Accreditation of Healthcare (USA; JCAH 1989) produced a comprehensive list of factors that determine quality patient care which draws from both Donabedian and Maxwell's dimensions of quality. The JCAH's list incorporated the following areas: *accessibility* (the ease with which a patient/carer obtains care); *timeliness* (the degree of care made available to patient when needed); *effectiveness* (the degree of care provided in the correct manner); *appropriateness* (the degree of care received matches the needs of the patient); *efficacy* (the degree to which a service has the potential to meet the need for which used); *efficiency* (the degree to which care received has the desired effect with minimum effort, expense or waste); *continuity* (the degree to which patients' identified care needs are co-ordinated effectively between practitioners and across organisations); *privacy* (the rights of the patient, to control distribution and release of data concerning his/her illness); *confidentiality* (information obtained from or about a patient is considered to be privileged and cannot be disclosed to a third party without consent); *participation of patient/family in care* (the patient and/or patient's family are involved in the decision-making process, in matters pertaining to his/her health); and the *safety of the care environment* (the degree to which necessary spaces, equipment and medicines are available to the patient when needed).

Current approaches to QA would seem to suggest that it is the combination of methods of data collection, service and clinical evaluation, education and guiding training which influences practice and leads to a more complete QA programme. Health care organisations need to adopt a unified approach to quality programmes with a clear direction shared by the managers and clinicians. Clinical audit is clearly one such approach to quality improvement in health services, but it is insufficient unless part of a clear professional or organisational strategy.

Chapter 3

CLINICAL AUDIT IN MENTAL HEALTH

In chapter 1 we saw how the recent reforms have increased the emphasis on the accountability of service providers. However, within mental health each patient brings with them their own lifetime's accumulation of physical, psychological and social events (Green 1992), any of which may have contributed to their presenting condition and require resolution. Therefore, mental health audit is subject to constraints not experienced by most other clinical specialties (Hatton & Renvoize 1992). Given the complex interrelationship of causative factors and the multifaceted approach to treatment, it is perhaps not surprising that health care workers in this field have been prone to special pleading and have fought shy of evaluation (Krowinski and Fitt 1978, Ovretveit 1992, Green 1992).

Audit of psychiatric services in the UK has been rather slower to develop than in other medical specialties (Glover 1990b, Bullmore et al 1992), a fact that is partly explained by the difficulties involved in auditing psychiatry specifically. Such difficulties include the lack of an objective pathology to guide diagnosis, the problems of adequately quantifying symptom severity or outcomes of treatment and the widespread prevalence of a multidisciplinary approach to psychiatric practice (Glover 1990b) which, although preferable clinically, does tend to make audit a more complex undertaking. This is because the patient is frequently treated by a multidisciplinary team all of whom may, or may not, be making contributions simultaneously. It is therefore questionable whether it is possible or desirable to unravel all these different contributions in order to identify how the final outcome has been achieved (Owers 1996).

There seems to be a consensus (e.g. Hornby 1993, Ritchie et al 1994, Firth-Cozens 1992) that in the psychiatric field interprofessional collaboration promotes better results than professions acting on their own. However, "teamwork" is a rather loose concept and has an ethereal quality which belies the great difficulty practitioners have in operationalising it. Insufficient teamwork has been at the root of many of the difficulties with implementing the Care Programme Approach (CPA) and the aftercare of patients (NHSE 1996, Audini & Lelliott 1996, Lethum 1995) and the authors presumably are not alone in having worked in "teams" where it was unusual for practitioners to have more than occasional contact. In the mental health service studied by Olsen (1992) the absence of a multi-disciplinary model of care was the result in his view of "competing explanations of mental disorder many of which are diametrically opposed and go beyond the usual bounds of conflict theory". Contrary or "multifactorial" interpretations gleaned from such candidates for explanation as the behavioural, genetic, familial, sociological, psychological and pharmacological (not to mention race and gender) are perhaps unique to mental health, with the result that practitioners are left to choose their preferences according to their own interests or school of professional allegiance.

To date in mental health there has been very little published that is multidisciplinary audit (Mallett 1991, Buttery et al 1994). This may have been because there was a delay of a couple of years before monies became available under the headings of "nursing and therapy"/"clinical" as opposed to medical audit (Cape 1995) although this seems in itself a rather unconvincing explanation of the lack of audit of teams specifically. There has been a lack of emphasis on the idea of evaluating all professional staff activity with this care group. Evaluative efforts have in the main been limited to the contributions of each discipline separately and most experience with audit is within each profession (Ovretveit 1992). Different staff groups each have their own professional norms and models of practice and review other than by professional peers can appear to be a violation of professional autonomy.

If it is correct that uniprofessional audit may be largely irrelevant and inappropriate in mental health because of the impossibility of separating various components of the service provided, then perhaps the main characteristics of an approach aimed at true multidisciplinary audit would be one where proper documentation, specification, measurement and evaluation of outcomes are essential parts of routine procedure by the team as a whole.

Glover (1994) carried out a review of all the articles published on psychiatric audit in the bulletin of the Royal College of Psychiatrists in the five years from the middle of 1989 to 1994 and found 83 published papers on the subject. Nearly half of these (43%) were in the area of general adult psychiatry but audit activity in other areas of psychiatry was also noted (learning disabilities 10%; child and adolescent 9%; Mental Health Act 7%; psychotherapy 6%). Most of these papers were not anecdotal but based on some kind of number analysis and around half of them arrived at specific recommendations for improved practice. Seventy per cent came from psychiatric teaching hospitals and 30% from non-teaching establishments and the content reflected a wide range of interests and issues including the accessibility of services, the use of services by ethnic minorities, processes of psychotherapy, and the workings of psychogeriatric services.

Popular "topics" have included the Mental Health Act (e.g. Rusius 1992, Feenan 1994, Wesson & Rigby 1994); ECT (Pippard & Ellam 1981, Pippard 1992a, Delany 1992, Robertson et al 1995); admissions and discharges (Hollander & Slater 1994, Tantum et al 1992, Jones 1991, Cowan 1991, Double 1991, Mai et al 1993); the elderly: including diagnosis, long-term placement for people with dementia, and service planning (Burn et al 1992, Reddy & Pitt 1993, Rands 1992, Feenan 1994, Shah & Ames 1994, Johnson & DiBona 1990); neuroleptic drug treatment (Warner et al 1995, Thompson 1994); lithium (Taylor & Dewar 1994); psychotherapy, especially behavioural and cognitive psychotherapy (Parry 1992, Denman 1994, Lovell et al 1994); and suicide (Morgan & Owen 1990, Morgan & Priest 1991, Rossiter 1991, Wishert et al 1993, Lelliott 1994, Morgan 1994).

Some frequently occuring "topics" such as the Mental Health Act and ECT may be popular for audit because these events are some of the few in psychiatry on which routine data have been recorded (Owers 1996). Other areas have attracted a larger amount of audit activity because of national leads or directives. For example, the interest in suicide audit was prompted by the Health of the Nation target for suicide reduction and the Confidential Inquiry into Homicides and Suicides, an exercise initiated with ministerial approval in 1992. Between July 1992 and December 1994 279 cases of suicides were scrutinised by the inquiry. The inquiry produced little evidence of any mismanagement or neglect precipitating death. One theme noted was that many of the deaths had a common factor of lack of compliance by patients to treatment and the services provided by mental health professionals.

Similarly, the relatively large sum of central audit funding allocated to the Royal College of Psychiatrists and its College Research Unit (CRU) has resulted in an increasing central direction as the CRU has undertaken an extensive programme of work and claimed the central lead within mental health (Marriott & Lelliott 1994). Parallel units have been established by the Royal College of Nursing (RCN) and the British Psychological Society (BPS) (the Centre for Clinical Outcomes, Research and Effectiveness). The principal objective of the CRU was to provide a lead on the development of guidelines, measures of outcome, and informatics in psychiatry. Wing (1994) divides this work into "top-down" contractual audit arrangements and "bottom-up" needs assessment. "Top-Down" audit strategies would move from national studies of epidemiology to population-based planning, cost of effective administration, continuity of care arrangements, adequate treatment settings, and appropriately qualified and competent staff. Much of this is analogous to the service quality aspect of "structure" (Donabedian 1980). "Bottom-up" audit strategies are characterised by the assessment of impairments, the delivery of best care for each impairment, the provision of care by staff capable and/or qualified to provide it, the correct settings for each intervention, follow-up, reassessment, and finally starting a new cycle (perhaps incorporating elements of both structure and process as defined by Donabedian). This is a considerable and ambitious programme but Wing (1994) argues that audit is in effect a hydra and that you cannot do everything at once.

The CRU has to date completed a number of multicentre audit projects in "priority" areas in mental health. Principal among these has been the Inner London Collaborative Audit project (Flannigan et al 1994a, 1994b, Bebbington et al 1994), which studied the use of acute admission beds in two London districts (South Southwark, and Hammersmith and Fulham; an investigation of new long-stay resources in 59 districts (Lelliott et al 1994, Lelliott & Wing 1994); the impact of the "Defeat Depression" campaign (Lelliott, 1994a); and a number of others (College Research Unit 1996). The CRU has also completed important work in "clinical informatics" (information systems to support audit) and in the development of "clinical practice guidelines". These will be further discussed in Chapter 9.

An early and perhaps most influential (in terms of audit) example of the CRU's work was the multicentre project on the administration of ECT (Pippard & Ellam 1981; Pippard 1992b). Pippard's study is special because it is one of very few which returned (completed the cycle) to look again at the topic under study. (A third study which will involve the re-audit of the sites visited by Pippard in 1990 is under way). It is a "clinical" audit in that nursing practice as well as structural aspects such as facilities and equipment and the ECT "environment" were included. It demonstrated major variations in clinical practice between two adjoining NHS regions. It demonstrated that powerful audit data can be generated from largely qualitative methods. It was also unusual in its candour and frankness. Finally, it illustrated the resistance to behavioural change that is a central challenge for the notion of audit and to the probability that such change may only be anticipated over a time course of many years.

Audit "topics" which have received most attention have been largely guided therefore by the availability of data (e.g. Mental Health Act, ECT), national leads and direction (e.g. suicide, admission policies) and local pressures (length of stay, over-occupancy). However, they have not been chosen to date on the basis of their fitness or appropriateness for multidisciplinary audit. In the remainder of this chapter we will address the kind of issues that might arise for study within a multidisciplinary context and the greatest determinant of these is the new style or "rhythm" (Glover 1995) of community mental health services.

Once the structural aspects of community services are in place (i.e., the Locality Mental Health Teams (LMHTs), new admission units, assertive outreach and "crisis" functions, day services, rehabilitation and work-related services and continuing care, long-term residential facilities and the like) it is the *processes* (Care Programme Approach, Care Management) that become the central focus for multidisciplinary audit (Jenkins 1996). Of course there are those who profoundly disagree that the structural necessities for community care have been put in place (Caldicott 1994, McCarthy et al 1995) and who therefore feel that the concentration on "care programmes" is premature and consistent with a "psychosis only" service (McCarthy et al 1995). Nevertheless, the whole thrust of community care policy (including all of the new guidance and directives issued since 1990: *Discharge Planning* (Department of Health 1989b), *Care Management* (Department of Health 1989c), *Care Programme Approach* (Department of Health 1990a), *Code of Practice of the Mental Health Act* (Department of Health 1990b), *Supervision Register* (Department of Health 1994b) *Supervised Discharges* (Department of Health 1994b) is towards the concentration of the service on the severely mentally ill (SMI) and the formalisation of teamwork to achieve this. Such developments could be seen as being in line with the redefinition of mental health care in terms of "biopsychosocial" principles (Schreter 1993), with continuity of care particularly being given a renewed status. Such an approach is one that focuses on the patient in interaction with the treatment system, that is sensitive to changes in the patient's condition, that encourages modifications in treatment in response to changes in the patient's status, and employs personnel who will modify service provision in accord with the changing needs of the patient.

In brief, the approach would involve the various disciplines stating clearly their proposed interventions with patients over a specified period of time. At the end of this period audit would be carried out to establish

1. whether the intervention had actually been delivered;
2. whether the intervention had been delivered with sufficient timeliness;
3. whether the intervention had been delivered to a sufficient level of quality (as defined by each profession);
4. what the outcome of the intervention was by an agreed unit of measurement or as perceived by the patient, his/her carer and the providing discipline.

We will consider these issues under the headings of delivery, timeliness and outcome (see Figures 1–3).

AUDIT ISSUES

Delivery of care provision

Ensuring high-quality provision of care requires an agreement on certain criteria against which the delivery of care to the patient can

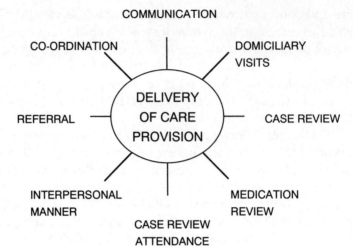

Figure 1

be judged. The degree to which the care provided fully meets the needs of the individual, which services and professionals are involved in the implementation of care and how the provision of care is to be evaluated are central questions for clinicians and auditors. Some of the factors that might need to be addressed are shown in Figure 1.

Communication: communication between various professionals and services working with the same patient.

The nature of mental health problems calls particularly for a multidisciplinary approach and yet difficulties have been identified between the two main statutory providers (health and social services), which have hindered the care planning and delivery process (Ritchie et al 1994). For example, health and social services have separate administrative and recording systems and the shared use of records between the two statutory services is unknown and complicated by difficult problems around confidentiality. Clinical information is usually exchanged between practitioners through verbal and written reports or feedback given in case review meetings of various sorts. It is sometimes difficult to identify what care is being delivered to individual patients by each professional agency or voluntary organisation and how often. Inadequacies in the exchange of information and failures to communicate can result in overlap of intervention, inappropriate use of resources and, of most concern, patients being "lost" to the system of care.

Information useful for judging multidisciplinary and multi-agency communication depends on the details provided at various stages of the care planning process. Obtaining information on a client from each discipline's case notes can be a time-consuming exercise. A central point for documenting key information or a common clinical record would seem the best method of overcoming such difficulties (Clifford 1996). Increasingly, in mental health, problems with communication flows are viewed as having an information technology solution (Knight 1995). The extent to which a service has effective communication between disciplines and agencies, particularly in a community ("dispersed") service, is a legitimate subject for multidisciplinary audit.

The involvement of patient and carer in the care planning process may be considered as a feature of good practice. Case management envisaged a much more active role for the user in devising and implementing the care plan (Department of Health 1995) than had previously been the case. However, patients and their relatives are often excluded from care planning whether in the hospital or the community setting. Service users (patients and carers) and service providers may have contrary beliefs about the degree of user involvement in the care. On such issues major differences of view about what constitutes involvement may exist (Gilles 1996).

Domiciliary visits: domiciliary visits by doctors, psychologists, social workers, community nurses and other professionals. The possible issues include number of visits, services involved, appropriateness of involvement.

In a community mental health service domiciliary visits for the purpose of assessment and treatment account for a sizeable percentage of staff time. Much of the intention of community care is to support people in their homes by providing more services on a domiciliary basis. With the possibility of a growth in home visits a number of questions are posed about their appropriateness and cost. What are the tasks best dealt with at home and what is the right skill mix of staff to deliver them? Are the number and frequency of visits appropriate for the needs of a given individual or group of patients? Do team staff provide adequate in-home support for the most needy and individuals with severe mental health needs? Do home visits prevent/reduce the number of crisis situations and the need for admission to hospital based units? Do home-based psychiatric assessments decrease the number of admissions to hospital and the use of the Mental Health Act?

The time spent by various professionals and support workers engaged in home visit activity, in particular ongoing visits, is an important issue associated with the appropriateness of visits and effective outcomes (Gournay 1994).

Case review: the need for each individual client's care to be reviewed on a regular basis. This would require standardised interpretation of how often a case should be reviewed and clear documentation.

The guidance on how to carry out case review and follow-up of a patient's care provision is now legion. The CPA, Individualised Patient Planning, Case/Care Management and Section 117 of the Mental Health Act (1983) all describe forms of care planning, itself the proposed solution to ensuring effective care delivery (Department of Health 1995).

The monitoring of whether care reviews are convened regularly, and the provision of criteria/standards about how often a review should be arranged, are salient issues to be addressed as part of multi-disciplinary audit. Other issues should include monitoring the follow-up of care provided for patients identified as vulnerable and/ or recorded on the supervision register (Department of Health 1994b). The level of severity of illness and complexity of needs would be a consideration when evaluating the requirement for sustained follow-up. A number of questions need to be addressed for audit purposes. Which staff should be present, and at what level, at a case review? How should information be documented and circulated to the relevant disciplines, patient and carers? Who should take responsibility for documenting and disseminating assessment, planned intervention and evaluation information? Once answered, criteria need to be clearly outlined in guideline form to enable completion of audit. The CPA Monitoring Tool (Lelliott 1995a) has recently been devised for this purpose.

Medication review: how often a full review of a patient's prescribed medication is carried out.

When a patient is prescribed drugs, whether in hospital or in the community, there is a need for a patient's programme of chemotherapy to be fully reviewed on a regular basis. Ideally there should be identified criteria to indicate how often a patient's drug regime should be re-evaluated. Furthermore, specific guidelines need to be in place detailing drug treatments requiring initial adjustment for optimum drug levels and ongoing monitoring (e.g. lithium therapy, clozapine and high-dosage neuroleptics).

It has been shown that the use of drug therapy without regular review (such as benzodiazepines) can lead to dependence and may have long-term harmful consequences (Tyrer & Owen 1984, Clarke 1989). Full reviews of prescribed drugs on a regular basis may be time consuming. However, time constraints cannot excuse failure to monitor adequately. The review of medication needs stringent monitoring for both cost-effective prescribing of medication and, more importantly, to ensure patient safety and effective treatment.

A further area of interest for audit would be the use of alternative treatments to chemotherapy. There is growing evidence that various forms of psychotherapy can be as effective as medication or better, either alone or in combination: for example, cognitive therapy compared to antidepressants in the treatment of depression (Elkin 1994, Elkin et al 1989, Evans et al 1992, Hollon et al 1992).

Referral: the process of referral and the ease with which patients are moved through the services in the provision of care.

Difficulties with access and the perception of being moved from service to service is a major issue for service users. Uniprofessional teams may have an established practice for allocation such as all new referrals being allocated weekly at a meeting chaired by the Head of Profession. Different professions may have very different procedures or variations in these administrative processes. This can lead to a delay in case allocation, assessment and service provision between professions and agencies which can seem very arbitrary, resulting in delays (for example, in the setting up of services in preparation for a patient returning home) which can be difficult for anyone to understand or explain. The introduction of community mental health teams and the emphasis on a "single point" of referral and case allocation by a single manager has been at least in part aimed at resolving these problems. Delays in referral can result in the development of crisis situations and on occasion can lead to patients requiring hospitalisation, when the need for admission could have been prevented.

The development and review of referral systems is important in service delivery, and common agreement on standards between services on, for example, response times for urgent and non-urgent referrals is an important issue for audit of the administrative systems which have been agreed.

Co-ordination: the extent that key workers and other disciplines are aware of all interventions implemented by other members of the team.

The organisation of care planning and the contributions of various health and social service agencies is one of the most important components of providing care. The use of terms such as named nurse, key worker, case/care manager, care co-ordinator and their defined role have been detailed in a number of circulars and reports produced by the Department of Health, most recently in *Building Bridges* (Department of Health 1995). These various titles and the roles implied by them are as yet unclear, as are any professional and legal responsibilities which may be attached to them (Gupta 1995). The co-ordination of care requires clearly defined roles in both community and hospital-based areas. The key worker is seen as being the linchpin of the CPA. He or she has responsibility for co-ordinating care, keeping in touch with the patient, ensuring that the care plans are delivered and calling for reviews of the plan when required. The caseloads of key workers have to be carefully managed and of course they need training. There should be no assumption that the key worker should always be a mental health nurse or a social worker although in practice they often will be. The key worker will be monitoring the care plan on a regular basis. The extent to which such arrangements achieve their goal is an important subject for audit (Gupta 1996).

Case review attendance: the representation of each service attending case reviews and how often.

Health and social work staff spend a great deal of their time attending care planning meetings. However, the numerous meetings convened to plan care often overlap with other meetings (such as ward round reviews) serving the same purpose and often reviewing the same cases. There is an issue of how such new forms of care review clash with traditional ward round practice. The work plans of all professionals need to reflect these priorities.

The attendance of professionals at meetings to discuss care programmes is influenced by a number of factors such as time constraints, large caseloads, unecessary meetings, internal and organisational politics, local policy and government legislation (Lethem 1995). These constraints may need to be considered when auditing care review attendance. This point was clearly exemplified in Lethem's (1995) study of 117 aftercare meetings. She found that meeting attendance by key professionals (social workers and community psychiatric nurses) was very poor. Due to the multidisciplinary nature of mental health there may be an assumption that team meetings to agree a plan of care is a practice which is a national norm. However, studies have shown that often very few key staff attend meetings for discharge planning (Cowan 1991) and Section 117 aftercare (Lethem 1995).

Interpersonal manner: friendliness, courtesy, respect, sensitivity; includes aspects of the way staff relate to patients/carers.

The introduction of the internal market produced a move towards obtaining consumer views on service provision and how staff dealt with patients and their relatives. The lack of concern demonstrated by health authorities prior to 1989 in obtaining the views of customers using the service was an important impetus for change. Services were planned by the authorities with little or no involvement by the service users. Consequently the service provided often did not cater adequately for user needs and fell short of providing accessible user-friendly services (Griffiths 1983).

One pertinent issue that is known to be of particular concern to users is their personal interactions with service staff (Balogh et al 1996). Each profession has a duty to practise to the standard of their own professional body's code of conduct such as UK Central Council for Nursing (UKCC), British Psychological Society (BPS), Royal College of Psychiatrists (RCP). If service representatives have no professional guidelines to direct their conduct it is important for each authority to have some form of guidelines and standards for staff to follow in their manner of behaviour towards service users.

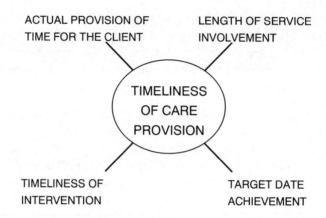

Figure 2

These guidelines and standards should provide the basis for audit. The guidelines for conduct provided by professional bodies and/or local authorities could also be used for audit purposes.

Timeliness of care provision (see Figure 2)

Length of service involvement: the time in which the patient is in contact with the services. The time the patient spends hospitalised.

Service interventions must be purposeful and delivered for the length of time that the patient needs them if they are to be cost-effective. For example, a patient should not be in a hospital admission unit if the patient no longer requires that service. The Royal College of Psychiatrists (1992) reported that often patients are admitted and cannot be discharged (despite completion of treatment) despite high bed occupancy and community care pressures – an issue of both appropriateness and cost.

Equally it is important that the patient remains in hospital for the optimum length of time that is regarded necessary for treatment so that unnecessary readmissions following discharge can be mini-mised. The reasons for extended and unnecessary lengths of stay in hospital are complex. However, it is known that unmet residential need is a major factor for new long-stay patients and that this problem is compounded by increasing rates of admission, shorter lengths of stay and an increase in readmissions (Lelliott & Wing 1994). Recent studies provide evidence for a concerning trend of reduced bed provision, increased bed usage, a shorter length of stay (due to pressures on the number of beds), early discharge, possible ineffective treatment and consequent unnecessary readmission, leading to increased bed usage pressures (Hollander & Slater 1994, Lelliott & Wing 1994). Studies of bed use tend to be retrospective and based on census methods (Lelliott & Strathdee 1992) and there is an argument that audit needs to be conducted concurrently (routinely) to enable a constant monitoring for the purposes of both effective management and service planning.

Equally relevant to this issue is the length of time community services should be providing care to individuals and what exactly is an "episode of care" in mental health. Should, for example, some patients never be discharged from the service because of their continuing need for maintenance? Questions arise such as: how long should a service be involved? How often should the service be involved? What is the purpose of the involvement? Could another less costly service provide the intervention required? Such matters require further basic research. Home-based and hospital-based approaches to care have been investigated and the cost of problem-orientated home-based care and standard inpatient care compared (Knapp et al 1994, Marks et al 1994). The findings indicate that the problem-orientated home-based approach to care was more cost-effective than standard inpatient hospital care, but it remains to be seen whether research-based optimism can be translated into ordinary practice, and local audit and service evaluation could provide the means for such clarification.

Target date achievement: This can be described as the completion of planned interventions by health and social service disciplines by an agreed target date.

The achievement of target dates might be considered another important aspect of a "timely" service. When planning care for a patient, the professionals and others involved may agree to complete a number of interventions such as assessments, therapies, organising of other services, domiciliary visits, contacting and liaising with other agencies and so on. The interventions offered may be high quality but may not be immediately available and once started may not have any natural "completion" date. Delays in assessments could lead to an increase in the total time needed for the service to be given as the intervention arrives not when the patient needs it but some time after. Reasons given for these delays are lost in the general working day and with it any opportunity to detail trends in delayed interventions. Without any form of monitoring it is difficult to establish a means of evaluating the completion of planned intervention and the time taken to complete various reports/ assessments.

Setting target dates following agreement of planned interventions can provide useful prompts to ensure interventions are completed on time. However, the introduction of intervention target dates may be opposed by both health and social service staff (see Chapter 6). It is sometimes difficult for individuals/teams to see the benefits of target dating interventions and its introduction may require considerable efforts explaining the putative benefits to team members. Fundamentally, the function of audit here is to allow teams to monitor their own services and to develop the care delivery process to best fit the needs of the local population being served by the team.

Timeliness of intervention: *client and service interpretation of speed of intervention of services.*

The most common service response to delays in service provision is the use of waiting lists. The reduction of waiting time is a central element of the Patients' Charter and one of the main causes of user dissatisfaction with mental health services (Jones & Lodge 1991).

Within mental health the problem of waiting lists is often associated with specialised mental health services such as clinical psychology and psychotherapy. A number of proposed interventions have been suggested to manage waiting lists. Approaches have included pre-therapy individual/group screening, use of brief psychotherapy/ intervention, assessment appointments prior to being placed on the waiting list, restricting access to the service, group work, opt-in/out systems, prioritising and referring on, training workshops (staff/ clients), telephone consultations and the provision of information (Malan 1976, Ley & Morris 1984, Christie & Francis 1987, Newnes 1988, Barkham & Shapiro 1989, Ryle 1990, Morrison 1991, Seager &

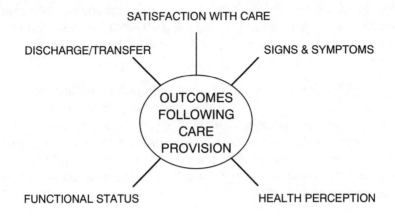

Figure 3

Jacobson 1991, White 1992, Division of Clinical Psychology 1993, Startup 1994, Shawe-Taylor et al 1994, Naik & Lee 1994). Little is known about the effectiveness of these approaches and whether waiting lists are reduced as a direct result of using them either singly or in combination (Shawe-Taylor et al 1994). Referrals and increasing waiting lists can be self-limiting (Kat 1993). Referral agents often stop requesting services after acknowledging that a waiting list exists (Startup 1994).

Outcomes following care provision (see Figure 3)

Many authors have commented on the particular difficulty of measuring outcomes in mental health services (Roy 1991, Marriott & Lelliott 1994). Outcome measures are necessary to judge the success of a service in meeting mental health need. However, with perhaps the exception of the recognition of "unmet need" (Gath 1991) there is no great consensus on what other outcome measures are relevant. Symptom measurement may be a necessary but not sufficient condition. There are few reliable indicators and it is unclear whether global or specific rating scales are to be preferred (Jenkins 1990). The optimal timing of outcome measures is uncertain as mental disorders may last over very long periods of time. This is prior to consideration of more intangible concepts such as quality of life or "capacity for relationships". Most outcome studies of treatment or intervention are based on the use of random controlled trials but it is the outcome of routine care that is of interest in understanding the relationship between health care delivery and outcome.

Wing (1992) nominated a number of outcome indicators for measuring the impact of a service, including reductions in excess mortality rates and of morbidity and disablement at both primary care and specialist levels of service, in addition to increasing quality of life and other district and national administrative targets. Jenkins (1990) lists the most commonly used outcome indicators in health care currently as follows:

- mortality
- morbidity (as measured by disability days, bed days, restricted activity days, or hospital admission figures)
- subjective health indicators
- direct measures of health and social functioning
- measures of unmet need

Mortality is the most frequently used measure. This has some limitations in mental health and is limited as an outcome measure. Morbidity may reflect many conditions other than health; bed usage and hospital admission/discharge figures are not in themselves outcome indicators because they are affected not only by the availability of beds but also by other factors. They are also very hospital based.

Subjective health indicators focus on experiential aspects of illness and distress and are important to consider because of the research evidence that self-perceived health correlates with rate of recovery even after controlling for objective measures of health. There is often a disparity between judgements of professionals and lay people on whether a particular treatment has been successful and it is crucial to take the lay view as well as the medical view.

Direct measures of health and social functioning have by far the strongest conceptual basis as relevant indicators of health outcomes. It may be possible to measure outcomes reliably in terms of symptoms (Dean & Foster 1988) but such measures are often lengthy and inappropriate to routine practice. The need exists for a short standardised scale to be used at regular intervals which measures symptom reduction and quality of life and which helps in the monitoring of routine care (Wing et al 1994).

Signs, symptoms and functional status: improvement/deterioration: were the client's symptoms/problems or function improved following service intervention?

The estimation of clinical outcomes in terms of symptom change has received much interest in the published literature. A number of areas of clinical practice were reported to benefit from health status measurement. These areas include the screening and monitoring of disease progression, improving doctor–patient communication and the assessment of the appropriateness of the quality of care (Jenkinson, 1994). However, can clinical outcomes be successfully estimated by monitoring symptom change alone? The answer to this question is definitely no. Factors associated with the health and well-being of a person are related to much broader issues than just changing symptoms in a positive direction. There are psychological and social factors to consider as well as the physical domain. An improvement in the underlying disease process does not necessarily improve patients' health and well-being (Jones 1992) and patients can feel subjective improvements in well-being without any changes at all in underlying pathology. Sometimes even merely an absence of deterioration could be seen as a positive outcome.

The use of symptom checklists as measures of clinical outcome will be discussed in Chapter 7, including the development of the Health of the Nation Outcome Scales (HoNOS). The HoNOS was developed to be used nationally for audit purposes and with regard to the Health of the Nation strategy to improve the health and social functioning of mentally ill people in ways that can be measured (Wing et al 1994).

Discharge/transfer: what happened to the patient? Where was their discharge/transfer destination (part III, home, continuing care)? Was their placement appropriate and were adequate arrangements for support and follow-up planned and implemented?

The effects of untimely discharge were discussed above. Early discharge can lead to readmission and other more serious outcomes, and guidance and good practice stipulate that patients should not be discharged unless they are ready and have an appropriate aftercare plan (Department of Health 1995, Royal College of Psychiatrists 1992). Failed discharges are the cause of the high percentage of patients readmitted with the same symptoms within three months of discharge for various reasons (Marks 1977, Jones 1991). Failure to comply with treatment or follow-up arrangements is common, and the response of the community services lacking in "assertiveness" (Jones 1991, Ritchie et al 1994).

The discharge or transfer of patients with long-term needs provides another area for potential audit. The impact of reprovision transfer can be deleterious for the patient, particularly for those who are elderly. An increase in mortality has been found to be associated with moving patients from large institutions to community environments following years of residing in large institutional hospitals. Similarly, the transfer of elderly patients to long-stay care can result in rapid deterioration in a patient's physical and psychological health status. The destination of patients on discharge/transfer following treatment or other intervention requires a great deal of planning. If the person is inappropriately placed the environment can have damaging effects on the patient's health. The monitoring of a patient's destination on discharge/transfer, follow-up and general provision of care is an important aspect of audit.

Health perception: the interpretation of the current health state of the patient following service intervention as perceived by the patient, relative/ carer, service.

The perceived gain in health of an individual following intervention by a service presents a number of difficulties, although it is recognised as an important measure of outcome (Wing 1992). Who is the most suitable individual to provide an interpretation of health and well-being? Is it best provided by health professionals involved in providing care, or by the patient receiving care or the carer or close relative? A further issue is how to measure health perception.

Audit of a service should attempt to evaluate its total impact on the patient. Validated measures of health and well-being may be one source of suitable summative assessments of the overall effectiveness of health care and will be described in Chapter 7. There may be a need to measure separately the often varying opinions of the main stakeholders on the patient's change in health status. The view of the patient receiving treatment, their nearest relative or carer and the patient's key worker are all relevant to the final judgement of outcome. Measures like HoNOS taken from the patients', close relatives' and key workers' perspectives would provide interesting comparative information for audit purposes when attempting to estimate perceived health outcomes in mental health.

Satisfaction with care: the client's/carer's interpretation of how satisfied they were with the provision of care by the service. Issues would include access to service, convenience of service provision and quality of the service.

The obtaining of service users' views on how satisfied they were with the provision of care received and their general treatment when in contact with mental health services is an important part of the audit process. Since the Griffiths report (1983) outlined the need for greater consideration of customer needs and views there has been a shift in thinking relating to service users' opinions. The Royal College of Physicians underlined the need to ascertain patients' views about the quality of care they received (1989, 1993). They outlined two areas that should be considered when assessing a patient's views relating to care received. First, the assessor should obtain the patient's perception of how much they benefited from medical treatment, and secondly, how satisfied they were with care provided. Both points need to be addressed by focusing on the broader issues of the multidisciplinary impact on care provision to successfully assess patient satisfaction with the care they received.

Obtaining valid estimates of patient perceptions of satisfaction with care is not necessarily an easy task. The problem lies with the collection of the data and who provides the information. Jenkinson (1994) reported a study where patient satisfaction was recorded by junior doctors (providing treatment for the patients they were assessing) and identified a number of problems. Results indicated a 100% satisfaction with the care provided. This was attributed to a number of factors: firstly, the collection of data; the information was collected largely from patients who were happy with their care. The patients were reluctant to make critical comments for fear of damaging their relationship with their doctor. Additionally uncooperative/or unavailable patients (taking their own discharge) were not included. Other factors associated with difficulty in obtaining a valid estimate of patient satisfaction concern a lack of time, inadequate recording, poor motivation and fear of eliciting criticisms (Warner et al 1994). The above points raise the question of whether it is appropriate for team members to collect information on themselves from service users. If various perspectives can be obtained relating to each individual patient's care the information can provide the assessor with a more complete picture of care provided and guards against bias. However, the process is more time consuming and may need to be undertaken by staff external to the service which is being audited (perhaps from an audit or research department). Safeguards must be made to ensure that patients and carers have the freedom to speak openly about the care they have received and their confidentiality protected.

Patient satisfaction is also linked to patient involvement in the development of audit programmes. The involvement of service users was recently reported in the development of a clinical audit project in mental health (Balogh & Bond 1995). The service users were involved in specifying and validating audit topics, as members of the audit team and as the subjects of data collection. They concluded that by enabling service users to raise quality issues practitioners can be provided with a rich agenda of quality improvement.

A unique difficulty associated with mental health is obtaining the patient perception of care provided to individuals detained/treated under the Mental Health Act (1983). Non-compliance with medication/treatment and a lack of insight, associated with a deteriorating mental state, can lead to compulsory admission to a psychiatric hospital. However, if an individual is admitted and treated against their will, what would be their interpretation of events following discharge? Furthermore, would their interpretation of events be valid? A study investigating patients admitted under compulsory order to a psychiatric unit found that the majority of patients were 'grateful' for admission and treatment when inter-viewed after discharge (Rusius 1992). The need to obtain a service user perspective of care provision is essential to the development of an effective audit strategy.

Chapter 4

CARE PLANS AND AUDIT

INTRODUCTION

Care plans have the potential to be the principal means of collecting information on which the success of a community service might be measured (Dean & Foster 1988, Wing 1992, White 1995, Glover 1995), for example, by assessing the extent to which the goals in the individual care plan have been realised over time. The individual care plans of service users should reflect the most fundamental aspect of the service which are the collective needs of the individuals receiving it (Knight 1995). In so doing care plans may provide a structured platform for teaching, contracting, audit and research (White 1995).

The value of more formulated care planning is that it may provide a reliable source of meaningful routine data (Clifford 1996). Providing information that is focused on the person rather than on the organisation or professional group marks a fundamental shift from the activity-based systems which have been historically used in the NHS. Part of the aim of the Mental Health Minimum Data Set (Glover 1995) is the establishment of an NHS "identifier". Most currently used measures (such as completed consultant episodes, number of patient contacts or average length of stay in hospital or Korner data) are neither individualised nor clinically helpful. Information is not available about the needs of individuals or targets for them and the extent to which the services meet those needs and targets. Therefore, it is not possible to ascertain how many people are using a particular service or whether the people who are using the service are benefiting from it.

Care planning should provide a focus for team discussion and a means of defining and communicating the key components of each person's care and for tracking it over time. Care plans may provide new opportunities for involvement of service users and carers in the assessment of their needs. Care plans have the potential of extending the functions of traditional psychiatric assessments by specifying more of the operational details of how care is to be delivered by providing descriptions of problems and objectives, planned interventions and who was involved in providing care.

White (1995) argues that, when aggregated, information on the problems/needs and care plans of service users may be essential for

- assessing care needs for the population served
- resource management (including staff management) and planning
- strong working between health and social care professionals
- ensuring effective delivery of appropriate care to the individual
- measuring the effects of various interventions and treatments for audit and research
- providing the basis of more sophisticated contracting.

The use of care planning data is usually discussed within the context of clinical information systems (Knight 1995). However, care planning systems for multidisciplinary case practice in mental health have not been widely available (Lelliott et al 1993).

A number of development programmes in codings, clinical terms and classifications, preliminary to a comprehensive information system, have been in progress over the last few years. These have included the Read code development project (Rix et al 1993, Wing & Rix 1994) and the common clinical terms project for coding and classification (Wing 1993), which involves the agreement on a national thesaurus of clinical terms and is due for completion in April 1997. The national case-mix office is developing health care-related groups (HRGs) in the field of mental illness. A new proposed minimum data set for adult mental health has been piloted in eight sites and contains the core information necessary to support clinicians in the delivery of care. The proposed data set is patient based and will incorporate components of care provided by non NHS bodies, and collection will take place in the context of CPA care reviews. In addition, the Functional Analysis of Care Environments (FACE) system of clinical recording has been developed independently over a number of years (Clifford 1996).

As yet there is no agreement about what items of information should be included in care plans. Care plans may include items such

Box 1 Coding Areas for Full Assessment Care Plans

Case description

Presenting problems
History of the current episode
Other psychiatric history
Current and past physical disorder
Physical examination
Personal/domestic issues
Case-related risks
Legal issues

Problem definitions

Diagnostic coding
Current case management problems/issues
Case management objectives
Outcome issue severity

Case management/interventions

Investigations
Case management interventions
Staff and their responsibilities
Prescribed medications
Discharge or closure management

as therapeutic targets, outcome assessments, when interventions are to occur, procedures for co-ordinating components of care, the management of anticipated risks and specifications of resource needs costing. Case management is increasingly linked to systems of management information, caseload analysis and service deficiency identification. White (1995) suggested the areas described in Box 1, which are themselves based on treatment plan specifications set out by the Scottish Home and Health Department (1990) and others (Lelliott et al 1993).

THE AUDITING OF CARE PLANS

For some time the issue of care planning and audit has been a feature particularly of non-psychiatric audit in mental health. In their review of nursing and therapy audit in England between 1991 and 1994, Willmot et al (1995) found that the majority of the projects and initiatives reviewed were in the area of "record keeping or documentation and the development of collaborative care plans". The issues had been highlighted in *Caring for People* and the Patients' Charter, both of which emphasised accurate record keeping and care planning – the former particularly promoting preparation and development of care plans and the latter given patients right of access to their health records.

Such developments have taken a bewildering number of forms and titles, such as "collaborative care plans" (Finnegan 1992), "anticipated recovery pathways" (Riches et al 1994) and "critical paths and care profiles" (Simpson & Brown 1993). Collaborative care planning, for example, is defined as "a multidisciplinary approach to the planning and implementation of patient care" (Solihull Health Authority 1992) which links outcome to cost during an episode of hospitalisation. Although these concepts are somewhat opaque, they all have the common theme of a single patient-centred care plan which is based on a care protocol (for a particular condition or "diagnostically related group" or process) which has multidisciplinary agreement.

Compliance in the process of care planning can therefore be measured relatively simply in a yes/no, achieved/not achieved format, enabling a relatively straightforward audit to take place on groups of patients on the basis of these agreed criteria. Such protocol-based approaches have been more widely applied in medical and surgical settings than in psychiatry (Finnegan 1992). What is clear is that such approaches have limited relevance to mental health as neither the diagnostic nor treatment certainty around the creation of such protocols currently exists.

There are a number of mental health systems which are based on the care planning process. For example, the quality assurance system (QAS), later developed into a clinical information system called "clinical outcome and resource monitoring (CORM), was developed by Marks and reported by Bullmore et al (1992). The QAS/CORM is principally a personal computer program for storage and display of problem-orientated clinical data, hotel and professional time costs of treatment, using outcome ratings and standardised instruments. Another example is Auto Need for Windows (Marshall 1996), which is a computer program for assessing psychiatric needs devised particularly with regard to the delivery of community care and can be used for audit purposes. A problems/needs analysis is at the centre of the system although this is derived by use of psychometric instruments (such as the Medical Research Council (MRC) Needs for Care Schedule, REHAB Scale, Manchester Scale, Mini Mental State Examination and others) rather than traditional clinical decision making.

THE FACE PROJECT

The FACE project has particular relevance to this discussion as it specifically focuses on how structure and measurement properties may be brought to the clinical record. The work includes a detailed assessment protocol for mental health (the FACE profile) and the recording of outcome information. The FACE profile was designed to reflect the clinical and social assessment carried out when a patient/client is first referred to a service. The FACE system is comprehensive in scope, containing nearly 20 000 items and covering all major clinical, social, personal and organisational domains. A major component is the record of results of clinical assessments to patients' presenting problems, needs and circumstances. In order for audit and outcome functions to be based upon routine collection of clinical data it is necessary to summarise data in a form that is usable for statistical purposes. In order to organise many thousands of items in a manageable form, the assessment system uses a multilevel, hierarchical structure.

Frost & Monteith (1996) investigated the measurement of clinical effectiveness in an acute inpatient psychiatric unit using a computerised clinical information system (Comment) and a multidimensional assessment schedule based on the FACE codes. The study took place on a small acute adult inpatient unit at University College Hospital, London; the ward had 14 beds and an annual turnover of 160 patients. All patients admitted within a six-month period were included in the study, which was undertaken because of the need for earlier identification of problems for "care programming" purposes.

The authors believe that this study demonstrates that it is possible to measure clinical effectiveness on a routine basis by a combination of systematic assessment procedures and information technology (Frost

1995). By analysing subsets of patients it is possible to identify presentation or management factors associated with poor outcome.

However, the auditing of care plans does not depend on computerisation. The auditing of care plans typically focuses on aspects of the process of care planning (for example, Department of Health CPA Monitoring Tool) rather than the content of the plan. Perkins & Fisher (1996) analysed the content of the care plans in a psychiatric rehabilitation service. The identification of strengths and problems by both staff and clients formed part of the routine assessment performed for care planning purposes within the service. Clients' views were ascertained via interviews and goals/targets set.

This enabled the authors to analyse issues such as the number of targets appearing in the care plan; the number of staff-identified strengths and problems compared to the number of client-identified strengths and problems; the overall proportion of staff-identified strengths and problems reflected in the care plan compared to the overall proportion of client-identified strengths and problems reflected in the care plan; the proportion of staff-identified strengths and problems in each area of functioning reflected in the care plan in relation to the proportion of client-identified strengths and problems in each area of functioning reflected in the care plan; and so on. In order to examine the extent to which targets specified in the individual care plans were achieved, care plan records were scrutinised for the extent to which each target had been achieved on a simple Goal Attainment Scale.

Perkins & Fisher (1996) found that it was possible to use the data collected to improve the quality of care planning. Most care planning systems employ some form of assessment process that involves getting information from both staff and clients. Documentation of this, together with a written care plan and some form of recording system (whether intrinsic in the care planning system or devised for the purpose of audit), are all that is required to examine the quality of care planning.

The latter point is supported by Green (1992) in a report of an approach to audit and quality which was put in place at St Matthew's Hospital, Staffordshire (at the time undergoing a closure programme with a reprovision date of 1996). The work explored the relationship between the processes of care and the resulting outcome. It was conducted over a two-year period by staff employed at the hospital on two elderly care wards: one an assessment ward and the other providing continuing care for people who would know no other home. The approach was based on a detailed analysis of each individual situation, leading to formulation of problems, priorities and goals. The extent to which these goals were achieved was measured against a baseline in which the individual patient acted as their own control, yielding in effect a series of single case studies as an indicator of progress. Further goals could then be established relating to changes in the patient's condition. As a result the authors argue that the patients had a better treatment and quality of life; staff attitudes were reported as having changed, and potential emerged for developing a system of audit which could provide managers with a detailed analysis outcome in relation to the cost of health care.

What these various studies have in common is the value they place on the routine record as a data source for audit. They are examples of care planning in a quantifiable form to which information technology and clinical information systems merely bring a greater degree of sophistication. Advances in computer and information technology allow larger quantities of data to be stored and accessed easily so that administrative databases can be expanded to include clinical information such as that contained in care plans (Garnick & Comstock 1996). However, it is a common mistake to assume that information technology is in itself the solution to team and multi-agency organisational difficulties. The idea that care delivery is enhanced by focused care planning procedures has also to be fully tested. Some assessments of procedural nursing care plans have suggested that they may not improve care delivery (Aidroos 1991, Yassin & Watkins 1993). Care for people with mental disorder often requires flexible professional assessment and on-the-spot negotiation of details, and care planning should not impose any rigidities which make this more difficult. The ethical issues involved in diverting staff time away from direct client care to provide computerised case management information also merits critical evaluation.

Chapter 5

INTRODUCING CLINICAL AUDIT

The introduction of an audit programme is often completed using the audit cycle as a framework (see Figure 1). The audit cycle can be used to provide a practical structure for carrying out audit. However, as noted in Chapter 1, the cycle does have its limitations. Not all audit methods fit this type of approach (Firth-Cozens 1993). Furthermore, the audit cycle and associated versions of the audit process (Fowkes 1982, Dixon 1989, Marinker 1990, Russell & Wilson 1992, Crombie et al 1993) assume that a basis for audit is already in place. It does not provide any structure for introducing audit to clinicians and managers prior to commencement of audit activities (Mockler & Riordan 1992) or allow for selection of topics for audit (Firth-Cozens 1993). However, a method of identifying specific health care problems as topics for audit was developed by Crombie and colleagues (1993) and built into a more detailed audit process.

In this chapter, we will outline a framework to describe the establishment of a clinical audit project (see Figure 2). The 10-point audit process divides into three distinct stages (see Table 1). Each of the 10 points will be discussed individually, detailing the problems encountered at each stage, and practical solutions for dealing with these. The stages form a process for the individual introducing audit to move through.

The structure was developed from two models for introducing change within organisations and teams (Lippitt et al 1958, Burke 1982). The proposed approach to audit covers all of the areas outlined in the original audit cycle. However, the model proposed provides a basis for a more complete description of an audit initiative. Furthermore, the process outlined deals with the early stages of introducing audit, the stabilising and maintenance

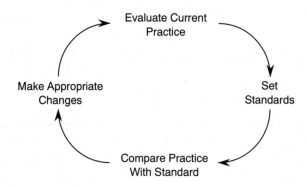

Figure 1   The Audit Cycle

of the audit process and allowing the "audit facilitator" to move on.

The model will be presented from the perspective of an "audit facilitator" (an individual with a lead role in the development of audit). The person may be external to a unit/community team where the project is due to be implemented or a member of the team. The process of audit would remain the same for either audit facilitator.

RECOGNITION BY SENIOR MANAGEMENT/TEAM MEMBERS OF THE NEED FOR AUDIT

The first stage in the introduction of an audit programme is to gain the support of both senior management and other professionals. It is important to determine the organisational commitment (senior managers/team members) to the development of the clinical audit project (Oakland 1989). If support is not ensured it may diminish staff's commitment to the project (Lavender et al 1994) and the provision of resources (if needed). The existence of government and health authority support for audit does not necessarily guarantee a commitment to audit initiatives at the team level – in fact the reverse may be true.

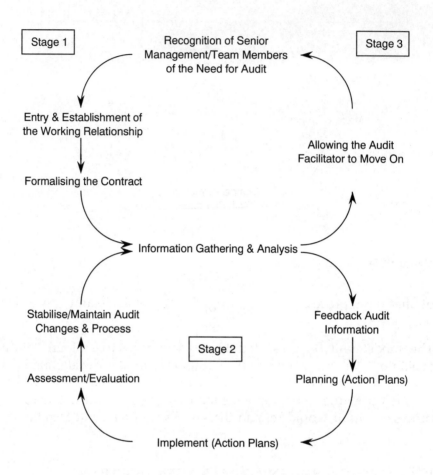

Figure 2 The Audit Process

ENTRY AND ESTABLISHMENT OF WORKING RELATIONSHIPS

Any project or audit initiative must have the allegiance of team members. The identification of a unit/ward/team to audit can often be difficult for a number of reasons. Opposition to audit initiatives is a common problem faced by audit facilitators (Atkinson & Hayden

Table 1 Stages of the Audit Process

Stage 1: Introduction of audit
Recognition by senior management/team members of the need for audit
Entry and establishment of the working relationship
Formalising the contract

Stage 2: Stabilisation/maintenance of the audit process
Information gathering and analysis
Feedback of audit information
Planning (action plans)
Implement (action plans)
Assessment/evaluation of interventions
Stabilisation/maintenance of changes and audit process

Stage 3: Allowing the audit facilitator to move on

1992) and this problem may be more considerable if the project involves several disciplines. Obtaining agreement from one profession to participate is often problematic. However, when consent is required from a number of professions, and agreement between both health and social services is needed, the problem may become quite difficult to resolve. Furthermore, the audit facilitator needs to determine topics for audit and seek agreement on standard guidelines, the destination of audit information and its subsequent use. These difficulties can be further compounded if the audit facilitator is external to the team. To reduce these fears it is important for the facilitator to establish a rapport with the team in the early stages, identifying key individuals within the team to aid the introduction of the initiative. These individuals may include clinicians, managers and enthusiastic team members who may act as catalysts for change.

Resistance to change may be due to individuals' belief that current practice is better than the proposed change (Nadler 1993). Some individuals (or groups) may actively seek to prevent the introduction of a proposed audit initiative. Active participation in the development of a project reduces resistance, builds ownership of the project and consequently motivates individuals to ensure the successful introduction of the initiative and provide effective networks of communication between the facilitator and team representatives (Coch & French 1948, Lippitt & White 1952, Vroom 1964, Kotter & Schlesinger 1979, Schein 1988, Nadler 1993). Atkinson & Hayden (1992) identified a number of methods for dealing with resistance to change, namely: education and communication, participation and involvement of team members, facilitation and support, negotiation and agreement and if necessary manipulation and co-option.

Before the audit programme is finalised, it is important for the audit facilitator to outline the benefits to be gained by the patient/client, team members and the organisation through their participation in the audit. It is often useful to be very clear about the reasons for audit. The facilitator must not be viewed to be serving their own needs or those of the senior managers (Eagly et al 1978). The audit programme should serve both audit requirements for the team and senior management.

FORMALISING THE CONTRACT

When introducing an audit programme one of the most time-consuming activities is the bringing together of numerous professional representatives from both health and social services to agree on standards or guidelines for audit to take place. This may lead to conflicts and can be time consuming. For each task (i.e., standard setting), varying the degree of participation can be effective (Vroom & Yetton 1973). For example, the audit facilitator or each team member could produce guidelines for the other team members to comment on until final agreement is achieved, leading to a reduction in time spent by professionals in lengthy planning meetings.

The questions presented in Table 2 raise a number of issues that need to be addressed at this stage of the audit process. Seeking agreement about what information should be collected, and team members' roles and responsibilities for data collection, is generally determined by a number of factors. These include national government initiatives (Patients' Charter, Supervision Registers), local requirements (for purchaser/provider managers) and subject interests at a team level. However, roles and responsibilities for data collection and internal/external access to information may lead to conflict between different professional and organisational (health/social services) representatives.

Table 2 Questions to seek agreement on

What information is to be collected? (Initial audit topic identification)

Who will collect the information? This may concern various members of the team involved in collecting different forms of information (particularly if ongoing data collection) and/or external auditors coming in to collect information

How will the information be collected? What measures would be used? Patient satisfaction questionnaires and/or interview schedules, collaborative care plans, symptomatology measures (pre/post admission and follow-up)

Where is the information to be collated, analysed and stored (and by whom)?

Who will have access to the information?

What information will be used for feedback?

Who will the information be distributed to?

In what form will the information be presented?

Would certain team members be allowed to view the information and comment before feedback to external (from the team/organisation) managers/purchasers? If so, which team members?

How will the information be used following feedback?

Working with various professionals from different organisations can result in competition for power over a planned project (Salancik & Pfeffer 1977, Tushman 1977). The importance of power and control associated with the introduction of quality initiatives and audit programmes needs to be uppermost in the thoughts of the prospective auditor. Conflict can also exist between managers and clinicians. Clinicians see audit as a matter of professional development, education and research, while managers see it as a measure of accountability for the used resources, and efficiency and effectiveness presenting a conflict of interest (Harmen & Martin 1992).

INFORMATION GATHERING AND ANALYSIS

It is essential for the audit facilitator to establish some sort of baseline measure of the current status of the service and clinical practice prior to any intervention. This information can be used as a comparator later following introduction of the audit programme to evaluate any change in service provision or clinical practice post-intervention. The baseline measure can be obtained either by retrospective evaluation (i.e., reviewing past interventions) or by conducting a small study collecting information over a short period of time – three to six months, depending on the type and size of the audit project. This need not hold up the introduction of the audit programme. The baseline measure of current practice can be collected while the audit facilitator is establishing agreement with the clinicians and managers at the entry and contracting stages of the project.

A number of problems may be encountered at this stage, including failure by staff to collect data, or incomplete information collected. These difficulties can be the result of a lack of adequate preparation prior to the collection of information. If individuals are unfamiliar with data forms and their administration, non-, partial and incorrect completion of data forms can occur. This can partly be resolved by thorough early preparation through discussion and teaching prior to implementation. Furthermore, the audit facilitator introducing the methods of data collection might consider demonstrating the act of gathering information. This approach serves two purposes. Firstly, the facilitator can be observed by various team members implementing the methods of data collection and then oversee practice attempts by team members. The experience could be used in discussion groups to deal with any problems encountered. Secondly, the facilitator may need to collect some data themselves to demonstrate his/her commitment to the project. It can be useful to produce some of the data collected for discussion to demonstrate how the information can be used.

Problems associated with data collection by members of the team may be attributed to the motivation and commitment of individuals and/or the team. If members of the team feel that they are collecting information to serve audit and/or managerial needs without any perceived clinical/service benefits they are less likely to be committed and therefore motivated to collect information correctly or at all. It is important to outline the clinical relevance of data collection, and to demonstrate the direct benefits for team development and service provision. Furthermore, educational and training needs should be identified and provided for prior to the implementation of data collection.

Following the planning of information collected the second component associated with this stage is the identification of methods of analysis (see Chapter 8) and the setting of databases/filing for information storage. The databases should be set to deal with the information to be collected and the questions that need to be answered following analysis. This stage is crucial, for if the databases are set incorrectly without any due consideration, the data may need to be completely reorganised at the time of analysis. When storing information without a computer it is useful to store information close to the time of data collection so information queries can be checked early. This approach should prevent the need to return to points of data collection (i.e., case notes, care programmes) to extract information following a prolonged period of data collection. Furthermore, early storage of information prevents loss of data.

The question of whether the data is stored and analysed by the team members using current resources in the team base is an important point for discussion. To fulfil the need for ownership the team should be involved fully in the storage and analysis stage, as at any other stage. However, this can be hampered by lack of expertise to complete analysis. The required skills may be taught or alternatively the information would need to be analysed externally. It is important for the audit facilitator to identify and utilise any existing skills demonstrated by team members. In some cases team members might prefer that the information is collated, stored and analysed externally due to time constraints. This method may be practically suitable; however, it can lead to a reduction in commitment and motivation in the project.

It is evident from the discussion that added resources may be required to store and analyse information gained from audit. Resources may be needed for computer hardware and software packages, including statistical analysis, database, graphics and word-processing software. Resources may also be required for secretarial cover and/or extra manpower to collect, store and analyse data depending on the nature and size of the audit project. The audit facilitator must pre-plan and identify extra resources required and associated costs prior to the introduction of the project. Funding may be sought from regional/local grants or from the senior management of the proposed audit trust/site. Requests for resources for audit purposes can provide a good estimate of management commitment to the audit project.

FEEDBACK

At this stage concern about the distribution and destination of information can become a central issue. Due to the sensitive nature

Table 3 Methods of feedback of audit information

Annual and/or quarterly report
Formal presentation of findings
Discussion through regular monthly team meetings
Large group briefing for combined clinicians and managers
Case studies in multidisciplinary groups

of audit information the methods of feedback need to be considered carefully. Information gained from clinical audit may concern various professionals from both health and social services. Data may be requested by managers in both organisations and by purchasers, including general practitioners and district health authorities. The release of information to various representatives external to the team without initial agreement can damage relationships between audit facilitators and team members and would also be in breach of confidentiality. For the reasons stated it is important to seek agreement between team members in liaison with purchasers and trust managers about what information should be released, to whom and for what reason. This may require identification and separation of information to be collected for purchaser and trust managers requirements and information to be used for professional and service development by the team.

A further issue may relate to the screening of information prior to release. A structure for the feedback of information must be put in place early in the introductory stage (at the contracting stage) of the audit project. Furthermore, information associated with the revelation of team or individual professional malpractice may need to be reported. This is not necessarily a common occurrence; however, when dealing with multiprofessional teams it is important to follow the correct procedure in dealing with this situation.

The methods of feedback of information should remain flexible. A number of approaches may need to be tried to identify the approach which best suits the needs of the recipients of audit information. The use of a variety of feedback methods also provides stimulation and can prevent the sessions from becoming too predictable (see Table 3 for examples of feedback methods).

The feedback of audit information should be well balanced. It is detrimental to provide only positive or negative examples. The presenter should seek to highlight both good and less good aspects of service. The presentation of audit findings should not be used punitively to criticise service provision, but constructively to stimulate debate on how to improve on and develop future services.

It is important to plan the organisation of feedback meetings (if this method is to be used). This would include membership, group aims and objectives, venue and how often the group should meet. Information may need to be disseminated at various levels. Therefore, meetings may need to be convened at a team level and a senior management level (possibly including purchasing representatives). Meetings should be kept to a minimum as it is often difficult to get team representatives and managers together on a regular basis, due to time constraints. Using only senior clinicians and managers to represent others at team meetings can reduce the need for numerous audit meetings. However, this method is employed at the expense of introducing a loss of ownership at team level, consequently leading to resentment, loss of commitment and motivation and in a circular fashion to a reduction in team efforts to complete data collection. This can of course work the same way in reverse if the meetings are convened only at a team level. The involvement of senior clinicians and managers is important due to the fact that they can allocate resources and can influence service change in relation to audit findings not only at the team level but unit wide. Some well-known audit studies (Pippard 1992b) may have been handicapped by a lack of managerial involvement.

The presentation of audit findings in meetings may be completed by the audit facilitator (internal or external to the team) or by various team members. The latter may be considered preferable in terms of team building, ownership and motivating individuals. Team representatives should be encouraged to present audit information that they have collected. It not only provides feelings of ownership and motivation, but also encourages individuals to examine more closely audit findings and consequently aid planning for change in approaches to service delivery. The audit facilitator may complete the early presentations and then gradually invite various team members to take on the role.

Table 4 Steps in the planning process

Obtain feedback of information from audit data
Review findings
Identify service/practice target areas for development
Set aims and objectives
Plan interventions to be implemented in relation to specific target areas
Identify what information needs to be collected, who will be involved in the data
    collection and how the information is to be collected (what measures)
Set time for re-evaluation

PLANNING (ACTION PLANS)

The planning of change in services and/or clinical practice follows
the feedback of audit information. The multidisciplinary team representatives may need to meet to develop action plans. The group
may need facilitating in the early stages to demonstrate the process
of audit action planning. The development of planned interventions
may be completed in team clinical audit meetings or by forming
subgroups or working parties with the responsibility to work on
specific areas of service development based on audit information
and providing feedback to the main group. The use of the main
group to action plan service changes would result in an increase in
the need for team members to meet as a group. This is likely to
cause difficulty due to time constraints. The small working parties
would only require a reduced number of team representatives to
come together to plan interventions. The use of existing meetings to
action plan can reduce the need for added meetings. A less time-
consuming approach would be the allocation of responsibility to
various individuals to draft numerous action plans to be finalised
and agreed upon by the main group. This would cut out the need
for numerous smaller group meetings and requires only one regular
meeting. Once the planning process is agreed the team representatives would work through the planning process for each action
plan (see Table 4).

IMPLEMENTING (ACTION PLANS)

One of the key debates in contemporary audit literature is whether
the audit process actually brings about any form of change in service

provision or professional practice (Smith 1993, Crombie et al 1993, Maynard 1993, Dombal 1994, Webb & Harvey 1994, Hobbs 1994). The successful introduction of a process like audit is dependent on the willingness of individuals to change aspects of their behaviour. Individuals who have power in the current situation may resist change because it threatens that power and therefore have a vested interest in maintaining the status quo (Nadler 1993).

The issue of obtaining resources to implement the required change is possibly a key factor as to why various audit projects have not resulted in positive outcomes. Examples of extra resources required to implement planned changes may include extra manpower, information technology systems and/or staff training. That is not to say that all change requires additional resources.

A factor which may be associated with influencing change related to audit is the lack of review of implemented action plans. Without any form of monitoring or evaluation there is no necessity for the implemented changes to be maintained (except for individual/team commitment). Therefore, it is important to set a date for commencement of the implementation of the action plan and its subsequent evaluation.

Other factors that may be associated with individual/group commitment and motivation to implement the change is unsettling events in the organisation (hospital/service closure) and conflict between team members. Any of the factors mentioned would influence the outcome of a planned change. These factors would need to be considered prior to the implementation of any action plan. Following agreement to meet to develop action plans the team members would follow the stages outlined in Table 5.

EVALUATION OF INTERVENTIONS

Whether using specific topic-based audit (collecting information over a period of time) or concurrent, rolling audit methods there is a need for an agreed evaluation date. Evaluation of the implemented action plan and the audit process used to bring about changes in service practice would normally involve comparison of present practices to

Table 5 Steps towards implementing the action plan

Seek agreement between clinicians and managers about what change needs to occur
    in clinical practice or service delivery
Decide what resources are required to implement the action plan
Obtain resources
Training if necessary in the use of new resources (information technology,
    machinery) or training of an individual to ensure the individual has the necessary
    skills to implement the agreed action plan
Agreement between managers and clinicians when the action plan will commence
Commence intervention of action plan

Table 6 Steps towards the evaluation of implemented planned changes

Follow-up of planned interventions at agreed time
Use baseline as criteria for evaluating changes in service practice/delivery and/or
    guidelines
Baseline measures (taken prior to the intervention of the action plan) can provide an
    indication of how much change has taken place following each review
If using rolling audit data collection methods provide regular times for feedback of
    information and review of action taken in response to the audit data and the
    positive or negative effect of the intervention

baseline measures/criteria and standards taken at the beginning of
the audit project or prior to the implemented change (see Table 6).

Evaluation may also involve reviewing methods of data collection and
the completion of data forms. This would provide information to be
used to plan further training and to monitor individuals/team
commitment to carry out audit in practice. If the implemented changes
did not produce the desired outcomes then team members should
work through the audit process again, commencing at the information-
gathering stage (if necessary), replanning, implementing service-
related changes and evaluating interventions (see Figure 2). It is useful
to consider why the interventions failed to bring about the desired
outcome. This can provide important information for discussion.

STABILISATION/MAINTENANCE OF THE AUDIT PROCESS

This stage is possibly the most crucial in the audit process. It is
important to reassess team representatives' and senior management's

motivation and commitment to maintain the implemented changes and more importantly commitment to the maintenance of the audit process. The process, once implemented, needs to be developed – it cannot remain static and must move on. If the momentum is lost then it is difficult to regain the impetus.

The facilitator needs to test whether the changes and commitment to the audit process would continue following the withdrawal of the audit facilitator. It is useful at this point to use a trial withdrawal period allowing the team to implement changes using the audit process independently. The facilitator would then return at a follow-up date to review the team's progress. The withdrawal process should be gradual, with increasing time periods between withdrawal and follow-up. The removal of support may not mean a complete withdrawal of involvement in the long term. The external audit facilitators may need to be involved to collate/analyse audit information and for consultancy, further education and development. The purpose of the trial period is mainly to promote independence and ownership of the audit process.

The withdrawal of external involvement in the audit process can be aided by the identification of key individuals from the multi-disciplinary team who demonstrate a commitment to the maintenance of audit activity. Individual interest should be encouraged from an early stage. Individual roles should be clarified prior to the withdrawal trial period. The assessment period can be used to evaluate individual commitment and performance in managing the audit process. Difficulties experienced in the trial period can be used for discussion either between or during the trial period with support provided by external audit facilitators.

It is important for the external audit facilitator not to involve themselves during the withdrawal trial period. The team members need to spend time dealing with audit-related difficulties without calling on outside help to promote the development of independence. The audit facilitator may also use examples of improved practice/service provision gained from using the audit process to motivate team members to continue with the implementation of audit activity.

ALLOWING THE AUDIT FACILITATOR TO MOVE ON

Following stabilisation and maintenance of the audit process in a ward/community team site the audit facilitator can move on to other areas. The use of a pilot site is particularly useful to develop audit methods for data collection, collation, storage, analysis and feedback of information. It allows for the development of a structure to disseminate information to internal and external agencies and for planning and evaluating services. Experience gained by the audit facilitator's involvement in a pilot project can be used to expand and develop initial ideas and methods to be used in other areas, possibly for a unit-wide audit programme.

The audit facilitator may be very involved at the early stages of the project; however, the facilitator should be gradually withdrawing from the pilot site from the beginning. Eventually his/her involvement with the ward/community team should be minimal, reduced to consultancy and/or providing a resource for data analysis and storage if necessary. The team members should be made aware of the intended gradual withdrawal from the outset of the pilot project to prevent any misunderstandings relating to the audit facilitator's continuing involvement.

In summary, when introducing an audit programme to an organisation there are a number of distinct principles to consider to ensure the successful integration of the programme to the working practice of the organisation and team. The audit facilitator must negotiate a clear contract at entry point and renew it as aspects of change occur, involve those who are going to be affected by the change as early as possible, analyse and assess potential for change, ensure support from senior management, target individuals from whom commitment is needed, identify potential champions of change, treat hurting systems, keep communication open at all times, use education and training where appropriate, monitor and evaluate progress and develop the facilitative role.

Chapter 6

AUDIT OF CARE PLANS AND THE CARE PROGRAMME APPROACH AT CLAYBURY HOSPITAL

INTRODUCTION

This chapter will take in turn two studies of care plan audit which were completed at Claybury Hospital prior to its closure in 1996. The first explored how care plans might be used at the level of a team or unit (an acute admission unit for the elderly). The second assessed how care plans might be used to monitor the activity and yield audit information for a larger unit of service (all the acute admission units within the service).

The intention of the work at Claybury Hospital was to develop methods for linking care planning and clinical (multidisciplinary) audit in mental health and to explore how to routinely monitor a psychiatric service through individual care plans and care reviews, i.e., documentation which had a primarily clinical purpose.

The care plan was viewed as the main vehicle for achieving this aim (see Chapter 3) as it is on the "care plan" that many community care processes (such as care management/care programme approach) are focused. Using care planning as a data source for team audit also had the advantage of not requiring the imposition of additional data collection paperwork as CPA was already a national requirement. In addition, as years of development had taken place within the Claybury service in the training of nursing staff on the "nursing process" and its successors ("individual patient care") it made sense locally to build on existing nursing practice by evolving such documentation into a multidisciplinary instrument.

There are problems connected with the use of routinely collected data, such as that contained in care plans, even if it is clinically relevant, namely concerns about quality and staff compliance (McKee 1993), and some have expressed scepticism about linking audit to CPA (Foster et al 1996) or indeed to any kind of routine data system (Firth-Cozens 1993). Locally developed information systems may have advantages over national systems such as the proposed Mental Health Minimum Data Set (Glover et al 1994a) or Korner mainly because "ownership" by clinicians will tend to improve data quality. However, the fact that data systems are locally derived does not necessarily mean that compliance will improve (Lyons & Gumbert 1990, Barrie, & Marsh 1992). Common sense dictates that data quality will never improve in any system if the data is not used. The usefulness of routine data such as that recorded in care plans has yet to be demonstrated not just for audit purposes but also for case finding, activity monitoring and contracting.

"TEAM" AUDIT USING CARE PLANS

The "team" study was initially funded from a regional grant from nursing and therapy audit monies and was carried out in an inpatient admission unit for the elderly mentally ill (and with the full backing of the mental health management team for the service). The unit consisting of 15 beds serving part of the catchment area for elderly people in the Waltham Forest area of northeast London. The ward functioned as part of a larger unit which also included 15 integrated day hospital places for the elderly mentally ill.

The team for this combined unit consisted of a consultant psycho-geriatrician, senior registrar, senior house officer and part-time clinical assistant. Nurse staffing for the unit comprised a ward manager and a complement of nurses. A full-time occupational therapy aide was also allocated to the unit. Sessional time was provided by a senior occupational therapist, clinical psychologist and social worker. The service also provided or had access to a variety of post-discharge services, including an attached day hospital unit, social services facilities, home care and community psychiatric nurse (CPN) services.

All patients who were admitted to the unit over the course of a year (a total of 60 patients) had their service delivery documented in the form of a multidisciplinary care plan. The average age of the 60 consecutive patients was 77.2 years (range 65–90 years). The sex ratio was approximately two females to one male. The average duration was 69 days (range 14–187 days). Almost half had a diagnosis of dementia (27) whilst the remainder had functional diagnoses (depression 12; affective psychosis 6; schizophrenia 8; and other 7). No significant differences in length of stay were found between patients with "functional" and "organic" diagnoses.

The multidisciplinary care plan devised contained basic epidemiological data (age, sex, diagnosis, etc.) and detailed users' principal problems, targets for each on discharge, interventions (assessments, therapies and services) given, service deficiencies which arose in their care, timeliness and delays in the service response, and pre/post measures of patients' symptomatology. Part of the task of the study was to devise clinical planning documentation and establish service processes around care planning that had the confidence of the team and which included users, and that might be extended to the hospital as a whole at a later date as part of CPA implementation. Of course, the existence of a care plan does not in itself provide evidence of care (Perkins & Fisher 1996). This must be tested on what is in the care plan and whether what is in it gets delivered.

The study established the basic processes of care planning which should take place as a user entered the service to a point of post-discharge follow-up. Briefly, following admission of a patient to hospital a named nurse was identified and allocated to the client by the ward manager. Care plans were compiled within a week of admission, when assessments were relatively complete. As the multidisciplinary team met regularly to plan and update the care of clients, documentation of care was made on to the clinical care plan. The process was integrated into the existing ward round and review meetings. Examples of care plan documents are given in Appendix 1.

No multidisciplinary care planning system existed prior to the study. However, nursing process and "individual patient care" (IPC) records had been in use by nursing staff for many years, and ratings of client symptoms and function were also taken at admission and discharge. For the purpose of this study a three-way semi-structured follow-up interview with the service provider (key worker), carer and client at two months post discharge was completed and ratings made of various outcomes (Riordan & Mockler 1996).

KEY WORKER RESPONSIBILITY

The plan was "overseen" by the key worker or "named nurse". There was no requirement that the key worker should be a nurse, but because on the inpatient unit in which the pilot was carried out the named nurse system was already in place, it was decided to build on this pre-existing and complementary arrangement. The plan was updated by the named nurse following consultant-led ward reviews. The named nurse was also responsible for discussing and agreeing the plan with users and their carers.

Following treatment and prior to discharge a discharge planning meeting was organised as part of the routine ward review. Members of the team involved in providing aftercare for the patient were invited to the meeting. The completed plan would then be copied and circulated to relevant others including the patient/carer, general practitioner, community key worker and the CPA manager. Ratings of the resolution of patients' problems were made by the named nurse in liaison with the patient/carer at discharge from the ward.

After discharge the co-ordination and documentation of multidisciplinary care provision became the responsibility of a community-based named nurse/key worker. In addition the CPA manager (a senior nurse) contacted every patient and/or their key worker at two months post discharge to monitor aftercare, record service deficiencies and if necessary to arrange further community reviews. At two months review further ratings of resolution of the problems which had presented on admission were made by the CPA manager in liaison with the key worker and the patient/carer. This joint review of outcome by the CPA co-ordinator and the user/carer constituted the completion of the admission "episode" of care.

Two months post discharge was chosen as a reasonable "episode of care" for the purpose of this study because such a time interval was considered long enough for some longevity of response to inpatient treatment to have been established, and to give some time for community services (or aftercare) to be established and evaluated.

USE OF THE CARE PLAN FOR AUDIT

It is a good clinical objective to ensure a clear delineation of problems, the interventions aimed at ameliorating them and the resulting outcome (Rutter 1982). Concentration on problems is part of everyday clinical practice and leads naturally to a pragmatic examination of whether best practice is being achieved (Leahy & Winkley 1992). Any care plan should list the presenting problems and/or needs of the client as specifically as possible.

Analysing the specific problems/needs with which users present moves away from the "illness model" of disease which is based on psychiatric diagnosis (Reiman 1989, Bullmore et al 1992). Definitions based on problems may also carry greater potential for user participation as they should be clearly involved in the definition of such problems and in describing their own needs. This is a basic tenet of the CPA and might be seen as representing a counterbalance to the predominance of biological models by drawing attention to the part played in the presentation of mental disorder by social and psychological factors (Olsen 1992). For these reasons the principal audit measures focused on specific types of problems identified and their resolution at two points in time (at discharge and at two months follow-up).

Problems identified by the team were of following type: "incontinent", "hearing voices", "overweight", "not eating", "refusing services", "lonely", and the like. The problems were listed in the care plan under three broad headings (physical, psychological and social; see Appendix 2). Problem identification became part of routine assessment and a list of problems together with strengths (anything the patient can still do, anything the patient used to like to do and anyone in the patient's social network who can help) made up for each patient a summary of the assessment. Much of the relevant information for this came from the interviewing of carers. At case reviews patients and carers were asked to agree to the problem/ strengths list, to comment on them, change them, subtract from them or add to them.

For each problem a desired goal or target on discharge was set. Targets for discharge were those considered by the team to be realistic and achievable (for example, "to return to previous weight", "to have an adequate dietary intake", "to enable mobilisation around flat", "to accept need for help and services", "to find more suitable accommodation", "to reduce the frequency/severity of aggression", "to reduce the frequency/severity of hallucinations" and so on.

Targets were directly linked to presenting problems and therefore the degree of problem resolution and the extent of target achievement in effect were identical. Service users and their carers were asked to rate the degree to which the problems they had initially presented (and agreed) with the team had resolved at two points in time (discharge and follow-up) as a result of the interventions given and goals achieved in their programme. The interventions planned by the team to achieve these targets were also recorded. Care plan documentation provided a record of what treatments, assessments and interventions were delivered in relation to the patients' problems identified on admission.

Data on interventions is needed for answering questions on both process and outcome of care (Wing 1992, Olsen 1992, Owers 1996). Interventions can take many forms, such as counselling, administration of drugs or ECT. The very basic requirements for outcome measurement are a description of the intervention and measures of the condition of the patient before and after the intervention, with the post-intervention measurement being recorded after an appropriate interval (McKee 1993). The main complication is estimating the level of "severity" of the patient's condition (Wing 1992). The principal diagnosis should enable us to know something about the condition of the patient before intervention. However, additional measures of symptom/functional status may be required to monitor clinical change over time and the user's perception of what had been achieved and their level of benefit is also an essential measure of eventual outcome, as nomothetic approaches are unlikely by themselves to produce usable results (Slade 1996).

Various audit questions can be asked from this type of care plan documentation; for example:

- Which problems are the most likely to be addressed (Perkins & Fisher 1996)?
- Which problems (from reading of the literature and from clinical experience) might be expected to present?
- Which problems do the team tackle most successfully and which the least?
- What are the most favoured interventions for each problem type (White 1995)?
- How do these tally with "best evidence" from the literature?
- Are the problems chosen most frequently those which the team knows it can successfully address?
- Is the team good at dealing with the most commonly presented problems and not so good at the more unusual ones?
- Do the targets and outcome goals relate to the problems identified (Conning & Rowland 1992)?
- Do nurses and other staff feel more confident in the assessment and treatment of physical disease (Olsen 1992)?

Example 1: Presenting Problems

Analysis of the presenting problems and their resolution showed the service to be strong in the biological domain. Medical problems, sleep disturbance and weight loss were identified commonly and promptly. Other, perhaps less well-understood or "tried and tested" problems such as family and relationship problems for which no obvious intervention suggested itself featured rarely, and there was evidence that the care needs of families and carers may have been underestimated. A total of 230 principal presenting problems were identified on 60 consecutive admissions of elderly people to the unit. Physical problems predominated and problems associated with affective disorder and dementia were unsurprisingly prominent. Forty-eight per cent of patients had a coexisting medical or physical problem; other commonly occurring problems (25% or more of the sample) included loss of appetite, loss of key skills, disorientation and aggression. Suicidal intent was infrequent. Problems relating to psychological factors, social programmes, carer issues, home-based care and self-care were infrequent.

Ratings of problem resolution were made by service provider (named nurse/key worker), patient and carer at two months post discharge (Riordan & Mockler 1996). Best outcomes were reported for symptoms of mood disorder such as loss of appetite, loss of energy and suicidal intent. Ratings of resolution for physical problems revealed significant if modest outcomes reflecting the chronic nature of many of these medical illnesses. The most modest outcomes centred on problems associated with dementia, such as incontinence, loss of key skills and disorientation. The outcome for aggressive behaviour was also rather poor and some major differences of perception of outcome between service provider and carer were found.

Perkins & Fisher (1996) in a psychiatric rehabilitation setting found that strengths and problems relating to psychological well-being were among the least likely to be addressed in care plans and the least likely to be achieved. Targets relating to mental/physical state, functional skills and finances were most likely to be achieved, whereas targets relating to activities, psychological well-being and family and social contacts were least likely. Similarly, in an acute admission unit for younger psychiatric patients Frost & Monteith (1996) found the greatest improvements in the areas of mental health, self-harm and physical health (state-specific problems) and the least in the areas of problem behaviour, interpersonal relationships, daily living skills and social circumstances (trait-specific problems).

The lack of social and psychological care, the infrequency with which these problems were picked up, the service-orientated approach and the needs of carers, family and relationship problems constituted some of the main points of feedback.

Example 2: Interventions

Through care plan analysis it was possible to describe broadly the nature of the treatments given, who gave them and specifically the treatments given in relation to each type of problem. Chemotherapy and medication monitoring accounted for over half of all therapy identified on the ward. Ward activities (a daily programme of games, puzzles and simple exercises), mainly carried out by the ward-based occupational therapy aide, plus group discussions accounted for over 30% of the other treatments identified. A cluster of other treatments, namely ECT, toilet training, mobility training, relaxation, reminiscence, reality orientation, substance withdrawal and individual counselling, were delivered to relatively small numbers of patients, aggregating less than 15% for the entire year's sample.

Nursing, medical and occupational therapist personnel were responsible for carrying out the vast preponderance of interventions: 73.7% (39.3% nursing and 34.4% medical); and 21.9% occupational therapy. The contributions of other disciplines including social work, psychology and other paramedical staff accounted for 4.3% of therapy delivery. Social work activity was largely limited to the carrying out of assessments (17% of all assessments) almost exclusively of patients requiring residential care. Despite the acknowledged role of occupational therapy in the assessment of activities of daily living such assessment was carried out very rarely. Clinical psychology staff were referred patients usually for differential diagnosis or untypical presentation.

Information was also gathered on which interventions are given most frequently for particular types of problems and/or needs. For example, in the pilot study the problem of "low mood" was initially responded to by the apparent treatment of choice, the drug lofepramine (given in 70% of cases); the predominant intervention for the problem of restlessness/agitation was the drug haloperidol. The problem of loneliness and social isolation was responded to predominantly by a combination of ward activities (loose occupational therapy activities) and the ward group. Questions could then be asked about the appropriateness of each of these most favoured interventions for problem type, in line with what was known about "best evidence" from the literature on effectiveness and perhaps in the future from agreed "clinical practice guidelines" (see Chapter 9). It was questioned whether loneliness can really be appropriately addressed by joining the ward group. Similarly, the rationale and use of the team's first-line treatment for depressed mood and agitation could be examined or listed for a "topic" audit.

There were a sizeable number of specific assessment types and treatments and interventions listed by the team, prior to the start of the study, as being available which never featured in the plans of any of the 60 patients during the year. These included art and creative therapy, drama therapy, crisis therapy, marital/family therapy, perception and cognition training, psychodynamic therapy, social skills training and "integrative" therapy. Only half of the various treatments and assessment types thought by the team to be available were actually used over the course of a year. The audit question which arose was whether those interventions were indeed available and if so why no demand was demonstrated for them.

Example 3: Post-discharge Services

Care plans are useful in tracking aftercare services to the point of care episode completion (in this case two months post discharge). Approaching half of the entire patient group of 60 returned to their own homes. On admission 13% had been admitted from residential homes for the elderly. In addition a further 25% were discharged to nursing homes and continuing care wards. Less than 30% of patients with dementia who were admitted to the unit returned on discharge to their own homes. Fifty-five per cent were discharged to residential/institutional settings.

Death rate (patients who died on the ward or within two weeks of discharge) was 10% of the total group. Death rate was highest in those patients with organic illness/dementia (17.2%). Accounts of death rates in psychogeriatric admission units are few and far between but this figure does not seem excessive compared with those reported in the few studies found which describe such data (e.g. Victor & Vetter 1989).

Patients discharged into residential care (40%) received no other community services, with the exception of day hospital care. Only a tenth of the patients received any practical domiciliary care on discharge, most being discharged into the care of relatives. Activities and social programmes such as day centres and luncheon clubs were rarely a feature of the plan. Only 10% were found to have a community psychiatric nurse allocated to them at two months follow-up. The principal means by far of post-discharge care was attendance at the day hospital attached to the ward, usually on a weekly basis. The integrated day hospital and ward was felt by clinicians to have many advantages in ensuring continuity of care and as a means for providing a regular "respite" for carers. Such data enabled the team to consider whether this model of care was the most appropriate and to discuss alternatives.

Example 4: Service Deficiencies

Service deficiencies are usually understood as an instance where a patient's need was not met or as the difference between those services judged necessary to deal with a problem and those services actually being delivered (Jenkins 1990).

Service deficiencies may also be understood as deviations or variance from protocols or guidelines for various clinical conditions or service processes which have been shown to be the most effective approach. Unfortunately, there are relatively few of these as yet in psychiatry, although a development programme does exist to deliver them (Marriott & Lelliott 1994).

In our study "unmet need" was the consequence of two main types of deficiency: namely, promised interventions which were delivered inadequately (delayed, in insufficient amounts, ineffectively or not at all) and anything which had the effect of putting an obstacle in the way of care delivery (principally bureaucracy, lack of resources and communication problems). During the period of study over 70 such service deficiencies relating to individual patients care programmes were identified and subcategorised into six headings (see Figure 1):

1. Failures to deliver promised services (interventions and services promised but not delivered; for example, domiciliary care not being provided as arranged, psychological assessment not being completed, accommodation not prepared at time of discharge).
2. Slow/delayed responses and waiting (delays in various assessments and waiting for services such as day or residential care).
3. Clinical deficiencies (for example, lack of assessment depth as patients with dementia were taken for a "one-day trial" at a local authority home, misapplied and insensitive use of "time out" procedures, diagnostic errors).
4. Lack of resources (for example, no transport, no OT available for programme to improve shopping and road safety skills, no day facility appropriate for pre-senile dementia, translation services unavailable).

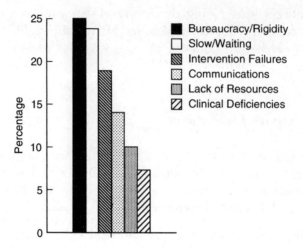

Figure 1 Types of Service Deficiencies

5. Communication problems (failures among team members to pass on key information; for example, occupational therapist unable to assess because patient never referred).
6. Bureaucracy and rigidity (for example, policy that a "crisis" must develop before emergency services considered, no places at day centres for people already in residential care, home care services only available before lunchtime, financial advice not available for patients whose estates are "too small").

Example 5: User Views

User views were taken at an open-ended interview at two months post discharge by an audit facilitator. The interview consisted of a series of satisfaction ratings which were in fact very favourable to the unit (Riordan & Mockler 1996). The spontaneous comments and criticisms of users were also recorded. A lack of information about and involvement in their treatment was the main theme which arose from these assessments. In addition, users (patients and carers) made sharp observations of their care, particularly in the areas of privacy, respect and interpersonal dealings between staff and patients. It is known that service users place a high value on the interpersonal aspects of their experiences (Balogh et al 1996) and user comments were some of the most "powerful" data fed back to the team. The confidentiality of this data to the team and individuals within it remained more guarded than with any other type of information yielded by the study. If quality of care is to be taken seriously, then it is the patients' perceptions which matter (Gilles 1996).

FEEDBACK MECHANISMS

The main methods of feedback were as follows:

1. Feedback on individual patients in the form of a short case review was produced for the team for discussion. These became formalised into a series of case studies produced as soon as possible following two months follow-up. The reports were largely descriptive, presenting specific issues which needed attention in relation to a particular user of the service. All aspects including user (patient and carer) interviews were presented (see Appendix 3).

2. Audit review meetings were held every three months involving the whole team. The feedback used all of the audit information available to the unit, which in addition to that described here included rating scales, and various three-way ratings of standards compliance and treatment effectiveness (Riordan & Mockler 1996). Feedback to staff on the unit contained the sorts of information already described above, with positive and negative aspects equally stressed. It must be said that audit meetings could generate strong disagreements and emotions and that the whole issue of how best to present audit findings is a complex one (Barker et al 1994). It is of course natural for providers to defend their service against criticism, however couched, but oppositional attitudes can be allayed given time and trust that audit information will not be abused. Focusing the feedback on the experiences of individual users of the service is helpful even when the desire is to present aggregate information.

3. Feedback to managers and purchasers was possible within the bounds of "confidentiality". For example, 70 or more service deficiencies from the study were presented, with the team's permission to senior members of the health and social services. Immediate

action on areas such as bureaucracy, some resource problems and service rigidities was possible and had an influence on service planning.

The pilot fed policy on new flexible forms of home-based care being developed by social services and contributed significantly to the creation for the first time of a social work team specifically for the elderly mentally ill. OT resources increased as a direct result of the work. With regard to the ward itself, there were changes in the structure of care planning meetings, a move to half-hourly sessions involving the carer throughout. However, the ward on which the audit took place was closed six months after the end of the study, for reasons unconnected with it (contraction of the hospital) and preventing aspecific re-auditing of the unit itself.

THE GENERAL STUDY

The study described above centred on the work of a small clinical team. The findings were "confidential" to that team and the analysis of care plans aimed at identifying broad areas for concern and subsequent action. However in 1995–6 the clinical planning system devised in the team study was extended to all the admission units of the hospital (with an approximate throughput of 1200 patients per year), replacing all previous IPC nursing records. All staff were trained in the workings of the new care plans and CPA throughout 1993 and 1994.

The decision to move the approach hospital wide was one agreed by the management team for the service with the intention of implementing further the CPA. However, the aim was also to assess how useful care plan information would be across a whole inpatient service and to identify what questions might be usefully addressed in the analysis. As the original funding under "nursing and therapy audit" had expired, funding of the work (one part-time facilitator) was taken up by the parent trust. The CPA was also seen as a way of maintaining service quality in a difficult period for the host hospital as it contracted to a planned closure date of 1996.

This was a distinct change in approach, moving from the auditing of the work of a small team using care plans to the auditing of an entire unit of service by the same means. In contrast to the usual "topic"-based nature of audit the approach taken assumed that continuous measurement is the only way to audit a large organisation (Moseley 1996). These ideas are perhaps more in sympathy with the concept of "continuous quality improvement" (Berwick 1992) than with the classic standard-setting/audit cycle model which has become so ubiquitous.

Accounts of modal implementation of the CPA are available (Millington & Slator 1995, Treadwell et al 1995). However, we found that it took several years of development for care plan completion to reach 90% of all patients admitted within the target wards. Only half of the patients admitted to the target wards actually had a care plan completed in the first year. In the second year (1 July 1994 to 30 June 1995) 1547 patients were admitted and discharged from the wards, for which 926 care plans were received (60% of all the patients), a marginal increase of care plans completion of 6.4% on the previous year (60% versus 53.6%). In the third year (1 July 1995 to 30 June 1996) 1142 care plans were identified from the 1268 patients admitted (89.9% of the total and an increase of 30% on the second year). It is not our intention to discuss the CPA implementation part of the process. Rather we report here on the uses (for audit) to which care plan data can be put. However, there is some evidence that the original timetable for the introduction to the CPA was overambitious and a number of reports have appeared suggesting that CPA implementation has been rather gradual (Gilleard 1995, Matthews 1995, Shepherd et al 1995) and on the same kind of time scale.

In the period 1995–6, the parent trust and the health authority identified the following items for feedback: referral agents; mental health act status; diagnosis; problem type; problem resolution; readmissions; discharge destination; services provided on discharge; use of service by ethnic minorities.

GENERAL INFORMATION

1268 patients were admitted to the target wards, of which 1142 care plans were identified and logged onto a database (DataEase) by

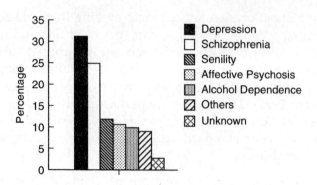

Figure 2   Diagnoses

audit clerks under the supervision of an audit facilitator. For the purpose of this analysis 1000 care plans were taken at random. The largest proportion of referrals were received from local general practitioners, accounting for 40.8% of all referrals. Large numbers of referrals were also received from other hospitals, principally the local district general hospital (27.7%). The mean length of stay for the general adult psychiatry admission wards was approximately 36.3 days. The mean length of stay per ward ranged from 32.3 to 45.7. For the two elderly wards it was significantly higher (76.2 days). Length of stay was reduceable to both consultant and ward revealing significant local differences on both dimensions. Diagnosis was categorised using Read codings (see Figure 2).

Of the total of 1000 patients for whom care programmes were received, 227 (23%) were admitted or held under a section of the 1983 Mental Health Act and these had an average length of stay up to a third longer than for informal patients.

Following their stay in hospital the majority of patients were discharged to their own home (78.3%). Elderly patients were less likely to return home (53%) and 27.8% of the elderly went on to some form of continuing care (nursing home or health continuing care facility), or died in the eight weeks following discharge. At two months post discharge care plan analysis indicated the principal means of follow-up and services referred to between discharge and this point, the most common of which by far was the traditional outpatient appointment at the hospital (60% of the 1000 patients).

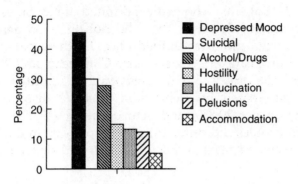

Figure 3 Problems on Readmission

Summary data from aggregated care plans can be presented on any aspect or group of patients, for example, by clinical condition/ diagnosis (depression, schizophrenia, etc.), by problem type (suicidal intention, alcohol abuse, etc.) or by category (readmissions, sectioned patients, ethnicity, etc.). As examples of the use of the care plan data two categories that were of particular interest to purchasers (readmissions and the use of service by ethnic minorities) will be briefly highlighted and a description given of how problem analysis and resolution ratings were used.

Example 6: Readmissions

Within the course of the year, 116 patients were readmitted, accounting for 148 readmissions in all (14.8%). Of these, 94 were admitted twice, 17 on three occasions, and five on four occasions or more in the 12-month period. Patients readmitted were split evenly between the sexes and had a length of stay not significantly different from those patients who were admitted only once. Of the patients readmitted, 87.9% were classified as "white", 6% were "Afro-Caribbean" and 3% "black African". The most frequent diagnoses for readmissions were, in descending order: depressive disorder (39); alcohol dependence (17); schizophrenic disorder (15); affective psychosis (11); and other diagnosis together amounted to 34. The most frequent problems presented by those who were readmitted are shown in Figure 3.

There were 24 patients who were admitted three times or more during the course of the year. They did not differ on demographic characteristics from those readmitted once. Of these patients, 87.5% were white European, 8.3% were Afro-Caribbean and 4.2% were black African. The principal diagnoses of those admitted repeatedly were again dominated by depression/affective disorder (37.5%), alcohol dependency (20.8%) and schizophrenia (12.5%). However, their problem profiles did differ from other patients in that they had significantly elevated rates of suicidal intent and delusions.

Example 7: Use of Service by Ethnic Minorities

Of the 1000 care plans analysed, 16.5% were from ethnic minorities and 83.5% were white European. Ethnic groups were:

- White 835 (83.5%)
- Afro-Caribbean 63 (6.3%)
- Black African and other 37 (3.7%)
- Asian 34 (3.4%)
- Other 15 (1.6%)

Comparisons can be made with the census (1991) figures for Waltham Forest (total persons resident in Waltham Forest = 212 033):

- White 157 824 (74.4%)
- Afro-Caribbean 14 421 (6.8%)
- Black African and other 9500 (4.5%)
- Asian 23 448 (11.1%)
- Other 6840 (3.2%)

From these figures it can be seen that Asian (Indian, Chinese, Pakistani and Bangladeshi) residents of Waltham Forest are significantly under-represented.

African Caribbeans are known to have higher admission rates and show evidence of higher rates of schizophrenia (Harrison et al 1988, Glover 1989), white Asians show evidence of lower rates of both psychological disturbance and service use (Ineichen et al 1984), although this pattern seems to vary between Asian groups (Glover 1991).

Patients from an ethnic minority background had a higher diagnosis of non-organic psychosis, although this was accounted for by the high rate of psychotic conditions amongst Afro-Caribbeans and black Africans (63% of Afro-Caribbeans and 66% of black Africans, and in both groups schizophrenia was the predominant diagnosis), whereas the majority of white European patients were diagnosed as neuroses and other (53%). The pattern of diagnoses therefore for blacks and whites is reversed.

In the Inner London Collaborative Audit (ILCA) Flannigan et al (1994a) found that black Caribbeans made up about 5.5% and 10.8% of the adult population of the two districts they studied (Hammersmith and Fulham, and South Southwark respectively). From population alone, Waltham Forest is closer to Hammersmith and Fulham in its population structure. However, unlike the latter where the number of Caribbeans amongst the admitted patients outstripped the proportion in the subpopulation by a factor of 2.9 (Flannigan et al 1994a), no elevated rate of admission for the sub-population was evident locally. Somewhat fewer patients of Afro-Caribbean origin were diagnosed as psychotic or suffering from affective disorder than found by Flannigan et al (1994a), where the figure was about 90% in both the districts they studied. However, our findings are essentially very similar in that significantly fewer patients were diagnosed as suffering from neurotic disorders and the great preponderance had a diagnosis of schizophrenia or other psychosis.

Taken together the percentage of patients from an ethnic minority background who were compulsorily detained in Waltham Forest was 46.1% compared to 26.8% for those patients from a white European background. When broken down further into subgroups, patients from an Afro-Caribbean and black African background had the highest rate of compulsory detention. Fifty-six per cent of all Afro-Caribbean patients admitted were detained under a section of the Mental Health Act (1983), a figure which mirrors almost exactly that found in the ILCA (Bebbington et al 1994). However, com-pulsory detention was even higher amongst black Africans (59.3%). The Asian rate was comparable with white Europeans.

PROBLEM ANALYSIS

Problems identified on admission by clinical staff were extracted from the care plans as well as their level of resolution, thereby giving an estimation of the effectiveness of inpatient treatment. Problems were categorised into three major headings (psychological, physical and social; see Appendix 2).

The most frequent problems, i.e. those identified in more than 50 care plans, were:

- Depressed mood 433 (31%)
- Suicidal intent 249 (18%)
- Alcohol abuse 182 (13%)
- Aggression/hostility 168 (12%)
- Delusions 155 (11%)
- Hallucinations 114 (8%)
- Accommodation 94 (7%)

A measure of problem resolution continued to be taken at discharge (by the named nurse/key worker and at two months follow-up (by the CPA co-ordinator). A simple three-point scale was used to evaluate the level of problem resolution at discharge and at six weeks follow-up. The scale consists of the following three categories of resolution:

1. Unresolved – no change in the problem.
2. Partially resolved – problem remains but at a reduced level.
3. Resolved – problem no longer exists.

Frost & Monteith (1996) used a simple four-point scale for assessing change in problems (resolved, better, same, worse), and for analysis reduced this to two categories: "improved" (resolved or better) and "not improved" (same or worse). Perkins & Fisher (1996) used a similar three-point scale in relation to outcome goals/targets (achieved, partly achieved, not achieved). Wing (1992) advocates simple number ratings of this kind as being the maximum possible in a busy work setting.

Such ratings enable us to see not only what percentage of problems were resolved at discharge but also whether they remained resolved at follow-up. For instance, depressed mood was resolved at discharge and follow-up in 60.9% of cases, resolved at discharge and partially resolved at follow-up in 8% of cases and resolved at discharge but unresolved at follow-up in 16.1% of cases. A considerable percentage of mood disorders were unresolved at follow-up, i.e. the patient had relapsed or had not fully recovered (24.15%). Problems such as suicide, aggression, hallucination, delusion, accommodation and drug/alcohol abuse were analysed in the same manner.

It is the capacity of care plans to produce information of particular groupings and subgroupings of patients that is one of its greatest assets. For instance, the outcome ratings on alcohol abuse were the lowest of all the most commonly occurring problems, with half showing no improvement in the presenting problem at two months post discharge. Two groups of patients – those who were rated "resolved" at follow-up and those who were rated "unresolved" – were compared on basic characteristics. The patients who were unresolved were somewhat older (average age of 45.6 years compared with the resolved group of 38.3 years). They tended to be male (2 : 1) whereas the resolved group were predominantly female (3 : 2). The two groups had the same average length of stay (16.4 versus 12.0 days) and the same pattern of problems on admission. Neither was there any difference in the type and amount of aftercare they received. However, the unresolved group had higher levels of both suicidal intent (20%) and previous admissions (25%) than the resolved group, who had neither recorded. Age, sex, prior admission and suicidal intent on admission seemed to mark those who were least likely to have a good outcome at two months post discharge. Such data can be used as a basis for a "topic"-based audit or for consideration of the need of these patients for higher levels of aftercare or alternative forms of treatment.

It was possible in such an analysis to relate presenting problems and their ratings at discharge and follow-up to the interventions received, although these were recorded very simply as follows.

1. Chemotherapy: oral (1), depot (2), Lithium (3)
2. Monitoring: mental/physical state
3. Counselling
4. OT and ward activities (diversional therapy)
5. Physical care, e.g. support/teaching with self-care
6. Nursing, observation
7. ECT

Table 1

Problem	Resolved	Partial	Not resolved	
Alcohol abuse	71 (39%)	4 (2%)	34	(19%)
Hallucinations	44 (39%)	6 (5%)	1	(0.8%)
Delusions	68 (44%)	12 (8%)	10	(6%)
Depressed mood	202 (47%)	19 (4%)	20	(5%)
Suicidal intent	90 (36%)	3 (1%)	5	(2%)
Hostility	51 (30%)	16 (9%)	12	(7%)
Accommodation	29 (31%)	7 (7%)	9	(10%)

8. Behavioural programme (anxiety management, behavioural contract)
9. Group therapy
10. Health education
11. Skills training (social, domestic, community)
12. Reality orientation
13. Seclusion
14. Psychotherapy
15. Social care

Like many studies of this kind staff compliance proved an obstacle at this stage of the study. As can be seen from Table 1 showing problem resolution ratings at discharge, a sizeable proportion were not completed and these were for two reasons: namely, the problems were present but had not been entered by the key worker into the care plan; or the problems had been entered but had not been rated. The table shows that 50.3% of the problems were given an outcome rating at discharge and 49.7% were not. Such a large failure to complete clearly weakens this data. A number of comments about this can be made:

1. Staff seem more willing to complete the "resolved" category than the other two. There may be a tendency for staff to record their successes but not their failures.
2. It is questionable how useful the midway rating of "partial" is since staff complied with this section the least.
3. Previous work strongly suggested that staff in any event consistently differ in their perceptions of outcome compared to users (patients and carers) and have a tendency to overrate their effectiveness (Riordan & Mockler 1996). Therefore such ratings need to be completed in parallel by at least a valid sample of service users.

4. On the basis of those ratings made, "alcohol abuse" was clearly the problem which was most resistant to the efforts of the team.
5. Findings from the team and general studies indicate that the local service seems to achieve its highest level of therapeutic impact on the problem of "depressed mood".

CONCLUSIONS

Unless it is known what a service is doing, it is difficult to know where to audit it. Care plan information may provide an overview of service activity and identify areas for meaningful "topic"-based or more detailed audit. Care plans are also a source of audit data in themselves and may identify areas and issues for immediate redress. The work described here is neither a research project nor a service evaluation in the traditional sense. The intention was to arrive at a workable system of care planning in a busy psychiatric setting and to use care plans as a source of audit information. It must be said that initial enthusiasm for this initiative (which was funded by a Nursing and Therapy Audit award from Region) was muted and it initially faced the kind of opposition described by Atkinson & Haydn (1992). At the time of the study the whole issue of CPA was a matter of considerable contention within the psychiatric profession (Caldicott 1994) although Olsen (1992), for example, reported difficulties in the introduction of "problem-orientated" care planning independent of the CPA and related government initiatives. It is not our intention to describe the initial objections by consultant psychiatrists in particular to this work as this would be tedious, but among the objections lack of time, fear of paperwork and incomprehension were all major themes.

The particular care plan devised threw up problems with the construction of care plans which required staff to think in terms of targets and goals in relation to presenting problems. This was despite the fact that many staff had years of experience in using individual patient care systems and the nursing process which are based on similar principles, that is, that all intervention strategies should be subject to measures of effectiveness in meeting their stated goals (Parry & Watts 1982). However, there are imaginative leaps involved in goal planning which many staff do not find natural or easy. Bullmore et al (1992) found that training staff to acquire sophistication in the task of breaking down problems into reason-able treatment targets proved to be a greater obstacle than the acquisition of keyboard skills. There is a need for continuing educa-tional work with staff on the operationalisation of outcome goals and behavioural outcomes which could be used as an observable/tangible measure of effectiveness. This training requirement should not be underestimated (NHSE 1996). Critical to the aim of intro-ducing clear objectives in care planning are the knowledge and skill held by professional staff.

Care planning must address all areas and span the health and social divide (Kingdon 1994, Shepherd et al 1995). Separation of health care into health and social domains is arbitrary and difficult. Much of the recent emphasis on bringing care management and CPA together is a recognition of this fact. It is certainly true that these studies suggest a concentration of the ward teams on psychiatric and mental state problems. The only "social" problem often listed was "accommodation". Perhaps this is not surprising. The study, after all, was on admission units and not community mental health teams. On the other hand, there are fears that mental health services (hospital and community) may be becoming "psychosis only" services (Flannigan 1994b, McCarthy 1995).

Clearly it is unrealistic to tackle too many problems simultaneously, so goals have to be selected against key objectives (as defined by the team). The type of problems prioritised by the team as the most significant in this study were in the medical, psychiatric and behavioural domains. Social and psychological problem definition was notably absent. In this sense the assessments of the team could hardly be said to be spanning the health and social care divide. Care plans are largely dictated by the assessments performed (Conning & Rowland 1992), and the lack of carer/family/social problems showed major weaknesses in areas of assessment other than medical and psychiatric.

There may be particular resistances around certain aspects of the CPA process. The CPA itself has taken several years to implement but over time staff have increasingly recognised the clinical import-ance of CPA. Features of care recording which are not perceived as so clinically relevant, such as attaching target times to interventions, recording service deficiencies and providing ratings on outcome –

but also by extension completing HoNOS ratings, entering data and other activities – will require significant staff and organisational development. It remains to be seen whether more detailed record keeping will win the approval of staff. Many studies report difficulty with general implementation beyond "pilot" status (Bullmore et al 1992, Frost & Monteith 1996). Although 72 service deficiencies were identified in our team study, staff were reluctant to use the forms drawn up to record these or to commit them to paper. A similar reluctance to be specific about deficiencies in the service was noted by Olsen (1992).

In this study no attempt was made to introduce comprehensive codings of the Read or FACE type. The advantage of the FACE profile, for example, is that staff are prompted by it to assess social problems in order to complete the record. It imposes good practice on staff rather than auditing what they currently do, which may be somewhat haphazard from an assessment point of view (Green 1992). White (1995) used over 400 codings in his study and Clifford (1996) reports 20 000 possible codings for FACE. With such systems there may be a danger of the coding itself becoming the predominant aspect of the service. White (1995) considers that the professional activities of his team benefited from discussions about which particular codings were relevant to each case. In addition, many services will be insufficiently resourced to begin to cope with such detailed documentation of care planning. A number of authors introducing similar but smaller systems have reported difficulties with staff compliance and co-operation (Bullmore et al 1992, Frost 1995, Green 1992). Nevertheless, a comprehensive and genuinely useful, clinically relevant and multipurpose information system may well prove its worth to professionals and win their active co-operation (Knight 1995).

This study is only an illustration of how care plans might be used for a wider organisational purpose. Among the weaknesses that can readily be identified are the use of staff-generated problems rather than using a formal system such as FACE, the very basic coding around problem interventions, the lack of any measure of severity, faulty timing (introducing the system at a time when CPA and supervision register (SR) were being actively resisted), the very basic outcome ratings (before the arrival of HoNOS), the absence of an information system, modest funding from a regional audit grant without any additional resourcing, either on information systems or additional staff, and finally attempting the work in a hospital which was in its death throes.

However, these weaknesses stem, at least in part, from the difficulties of introducing such changes into a real service with all its inherent chaos. Problems with implementation may be anticipated not just with services which are about to close. Compliance with comprehensive problem ratings and codings may remain a challenge no matter what their clinical relevance. Outcome measures, if they are to be completed routinely for each patient rather than on the sample or census method, will have to be very simple and "good enough". Training and staff development are always long-term objectives that are best implemented at the pre-qualification level. No system such as this can make good lack of basic educational skills and values if they do not already exist amongst staff.

Nevertheless, the care planning process has the potential to produce useful data, of which some instances have been described here. Not the least of these is that individuals can be tracked over time (potentially before and after treatment), large populations make it possible to select enough people with relatively rare conditions or presentations, and the Hawthorne effect is eliminated as researchers do not influence practice through data collection. Routine data from the service therefore has considerable potential for audit and evaluation and may have been undervalued as a principal source for audit in the past.

Chapter 7

METHODS OF AUDIT AND DATA COLLECTION

There are a number of approaches to carrying out audit. The following will review some of the more popular contemporary approaches to collecting data and auditing:

- Outcome measures
- Routine indicators
- Standards and criterion-based audit
- Case review
- Critical pathways
- Service evaluation
- Patient satisfaction questionnaires

OUTCOME MEASURES

The selection of health status instruments for audit or evaluation needs to be considered very carefully. The reliability and acceptability of measures of symptom/health status change need to be investigated and verified prior to their use (Fitzpatrick et al 1992). The following is a review of symptom/functional checklists and approaches to estimating objective attainment which have been used to estimate change following treatment.

Symptom and Functional Checklists

A number of measures have been used as estimates of symptom change. The Symptoms Checklist (SCL-90; Derogatis et al 1973) is a useful measure; however, the length of the checklist causes problems in completion. A shortened version has been developed but there were problems concerning copyright and the publication of the SCL-18. The General Health Questionnaire (GHQ; Goldberg 1978) has been proposed for audit purposes to estimate change following treatment. However, Firth-Cozens (1993) indicated that the GHQ is "not a change measure and cannot be used for audit purposes".

The most widely used generic multidimensional health status measures in the UK are the Nottingham Health Profile (NHP; Hunt et al 1981) and the Sickness Impact Profile (SIP). The Short Form 36 (SF-36; Ware & Sherbourne 1992), has become popular and is used extensively for audit purposes. An anglicised version of the SF-36 exists with the words of six questions slightly altered for use in community, and older adults in the UK (Brazier et al 1992, Jenkinson et al 1993, Garratt et al 1993, Hayes et al 1995). The SF-36 has an advantage over the NHP in being more sensitive to low levels of ill health, allowing individual respondents to choose between predetermined severity or degrees of preference and achieving a greater spread of scores (Brazier et al 1992, Hayes et al 1995).

Beck's Depression Inventory (BDI; Beck et al 1961, Beck 1987, Beck and Steer 1987) and Beck's Anxiety Inventory (BAI; Beck et al 1988) are well-used measures of symptom change. Another measure of depression which may be used for older adults is the Geriatric Depression Scale (GDS; Brink et al 1982, Yesavage & Brink 1983, Yesavage et al 1986). The GDS was found to be a useful estimate of change in depressive symptoms in an older adult with mental health problems (Riordan & Mockler 1996) and has been found to have high correlation with Beck's Depression Inventory (Hyer & Blount 1984) and the Hamilton Depression Scale (Yesavage et al 1983, 1986). Other measures used to estimate symptom change include the Hospital Anxiety and Depression Scale (Zigmond & Snaith 1983), State–Trait Anxiety Scale (Spielberger et al 1983) and the Global Assessment Scale (Endicott et al 1976), used in the HoNOS.

The HoNOS Scale

One scale which has been developed for audit purposes to measure change in a patient's health status is the HoNOS scale. The Health of the Nation Outcome Scale (Wing et al 1994) was developed using as a starting point the "Health of the Nation" target to "improve significantly the health and social functioning of mentally ill people". However, this deceptively simple objective assumes, firstly, a capacity to measure significant improvement, secondly, to specify what is meant by health and social functioning, and thirdly to define who are mentally ill people. The Research Unit of the Royal College of Psychiatrists have developed the HoNOS scale as a before-and-after measure of four classes of presenting problems in a 12-item questionnaire to be completed by staff. Parallel versions are under development for carers and service users. The type of problems incorporated include aggression, self-harm, alcohol/drug abuse, memory/orientation, physical well-being, mood disturbance, hallucinations/delusions, other mental problems, and social difficulties.

The group claimed that a new scale was necessary to encompass the Health of the Nation criteria and at the same time be acceptable to health workers, purchasers and providers whilst being simple, reliable, relatable to other scales and capable of routine completion by mental and health nursing and other staff.

The HoNOS scale is an outcome scale which has undergone lengthy series of trials and which attempts to provide a routine measurement of outcome. Originally there were 12 items scored 0–4 comprising a Behaviour/Expressive component (Aggression, Self-harm, Alcohol/Drugs), a Functional Impairment component (Memory, Orientation), a Clinical/Behavioural symptoms component (Mood Disturbance, Hallucinations, other behaviour), and a Social component (Social Relations, Housing, Employment). In addition a general functional rating of disability was scored 0–100 (Global Assessment Scale, GAS).

The aim of the work was to provide a brief, simple scale which covered clinical and social problems, could be produced in a variety of formats, would be acceptable to all professions and available in forms for users and carers. It would have to be reliable and sensitive to change and prove useful to purchasers and commissioners. By giving a measure of severity it could help with community psychiatric nurses' (CPN) caseloads and/or case mix. It could be a tool for audit and for CPA, as a resource use indicator and a measure of effectiveness. It might also have a place in contracting. The basic uses were seen as follows: case mix indicator, targeting/resource prioritisation, health and social outcomes, service effectiveness/efficiency.

By 1996 the scale had been very intensively studied, with 1500 of some 3000 cases having been tested more than once (Wing 1996). The 12 items were found not to be correlated with one another and a comparison was made with the British Psychiatric Rating Scale (BPRS). In the final version (HoNOS 4), some changes have been made as a result of the trials, and the total score has been dropped. It has only been used so far in severe mental illness settings but a HoNOS family is in development. It measures health, not health care outcomes (but it is an essential part of a wider data set).

ROUTINE INDICATORS

Data collection for audit purposes can be categorised into two areas: general ongoing or rolling data gathering of large amounts of information and topic-specific collection of data. The ongoing rolling data collection is the gathering of previously identified audit information continuously using care plans, questionnaires and symptom checklists at point of care delivery. The gathering of topic-specific data focuses on an identified area of interest. The subject area is agreed and then information is compiled, either current or retrospectively for baseline and then prospectively to provide a second measure. This provides information on a specific topic but does not provide information relating to broader issues of service delivery. It has been argued that routine ongoing information gathering for audit purposes is of little benefit (Crombie et al 1993, Firth-Cozens 1993); this is a debatable point. The routine collection of information can provide trend information to be used to identify topics for specific areas of audit and can be adjusted to collect information relating to government and district policies and information for purchaser and provider needs. These two methods of data collection do not have to be used separately as one in preference to the other, but complementarily, with each serving the other, making audit a live process in touch with ongoing issues raised through data collection.

Routine data collection may have many limitations but can be beneficial to clinical audit if it is part of a well-organised audit process. This form of data collection will never provide a definitive answer to a question about quality of care, but it has an important (and largely unrecognised) role as a screening tool to identify areas of concern for further investigation (McKee 1993).

The use of computers for routine data collection and storage of clinical information on a daily basis would seem to be the obvious way forward for the future development of the new health service to ensure collection of information like the mental health minimal data set (Glover et al 1994a, Lelliott 1995) (see Chapter 9). There is no doubting the benefits of using computer networks for clinical work and audit; however, the introduction of such systems can present both advantages and disadvantages.

The advantages are numerous: computers would provide the clinician, manager and auditor with access to a central point of information, easing problems associated with current filing systems whereby each professional maintains their own notes, making it difficult to gain a clear picture of the totality of care provided. The data would be collected routinely, providing up-to-date information on the current status of service delivery, practice and outcomes. It would provide an easier method of analysis and comparison with other areas if the appropriate software was available. The transfer of information would be easier if the systems were networked unit wide with various access levels based on seniority and maintained through access codes. The computerised approach would also ease the problems of illegible case notes and missing information.

However, computer systems do have their disadvantages. When problems involving missing data arise the difficulty is not easily resolved. This problem may not necessarily be due to system failure (although that is a possibility) but due to the non-loading of information by various professionals who either lack the skills, confidence or motivation to use the computer. Furthermore, a central problem is the maintenance of confidentiality in terms of access to patient details. Even with the use of access codes and various levels of data entry, computer systems can be accessed. When introducing a computer system for use in clinical practice the method of data storage and what is to be detailed need to comply with the requirements of the Data Protection Act. Other problems relate more to the difficulties that companies have in terms of developing large information technology software packages for mental health, due to its diverse nature. The new systems need to be flexible, to deal with changing requirements for data collection without requiring major time-consuming, costly alterations.

STANDARDS AND CRITERION-BASED AUDIT

This form of audit uses a specific number of criteria as a measure to judge compliance. An example of criterion-based audit was demonstrated in the West Midlands Collaborative Care Planning Approach, which used a detailed list of intervention criteria to be carried out by various professionals. The interventions were marked "Yes" or "No" as to whether they were completed (see Chapter 4).

Criterion-based audit can be used for various process and treatment approaches. Criteria may be developed by professional groups to monitor maintenance of case notes, completion of admission/discharge procedure, specific therapies (ECT, lithium), completion of compulsory detainment forms and attendance/organisation of care programme approach and/or other multiprofessional meetings.

Both retrospective and prospective approaches can be used initially to develop the baseline criteria from which to measure. The criteria may reflect team agreement, government policy (Patients' Charter) or local health authority requirements serving both purchasers' and providers' needs.

The criteria, once audited, can be measured against agreed standards; for example, if a standard indicates that members of a community mental health team must make face-to-face contact with emergency referrals within three days of receiving the case details in all cases, then the auditor would expect emergency referrals to be seen within three days in 100% of cases (i.e., on each occasion). The approach provides a measurable method of auditing current practice and change following intervention. Providing criteria and standards to supply a measure of clinical practice is a useful method of audit.

It provides structure, with something to compare practice with. Furthermore, because the standards and criteria are generally agreed by staff it makes them more aware of their practice activities and how their service is implemented at both a personal and team level.

CASE REVIEW

There are many examples of case review used in clinical practice and also for audit and QA purposes. These would include care programme meetings (ward rounds, case/care management and CPA), quality circles (Robson 1982) and peer review (Diamond et al 1975). This section will focus on the peer review approach to evaluating practice used extensively for audit purposes.

Peer review is a useful method of audit due to the easy adaptation of current practice to incorporate the approach. It is a predominantly professional activity that does not strictly adhere to audit requirements unless individual (or group) case histories are reviewed against specific criteria and/or standards. Following the introduction of medical audit there was some confusion over what constituted audit practice. This was due to the omission of the need for criteria and standards in the original working definition of medical audit (Department of Health 1989a). Consequently members of the medical profession continued to use their normal case review meetings, feeling the approach was adequate for audit purposes (Firth-Cozens 1993).

Peer review can be an effective method for bringing professionals together to discuss care/treatment interventions; however, in the long term the method provides only an introductory approach to audit and would need to be developed further. Consequently, the approach is useful at the early stages of audit to promote discussion, but would need to be either replaced or developed with the introduction of more refined approaches to audit.

The monitoring of adverse/positive events can be achieved using peer review, discussing good examples of practice and areas of concern. The approach can be used to discuss incidents of serious self-harm (including suicide/attempted suicide), acts of violence committed by patients (against team members or other victim) unsuccessful treatment or care intervention, complaints by a patient/relative relating to some aspect of care or treatment and other related negative adverse events. On the positive side, the team members may want to discuss a number of interventions and/or treatment which resulted in the attainment of desired outcomes, interventions which defused potential physical conflict situations between team members and patients, and successful planning and delivery of care through multiprofessional team meetings.

CRITICAL PATHWAYS

The monitoring of critical pathways allows the individual or team to identify key events to be completed to ensure the desired outcomes within the confines of resources. Northallerton Health Services implemented a critical pathway approach to audit (Brown & Simpson 1992). They described the process as a "multidisciplinary process of planning, documenting and reviewing patient care". They identified a number of key elements of patient care which must occur for a specific diagnosis or procedure and at the same time considers appropriate time-frames to be followed to achieve the optimum outcome for patients. The process is used for:

1. Ongoing identification of variations to the critical path
2. The reason for the variation
3. Any action taken
4. Comparing patient care with the pre-agreed standard

The approach sought to provide a method which minimises variations in clinical practice and for accurate costing of interventions within a care episode.

A more recent example of the critical pathway approach is the Clinical Standards Advisory Group's review of clinical standards maintained for people with schizophrenia (CSAG 1995). The group recommended that mental health services should address the following areas:

• Setting explicit local standards, in consultation with users and carers
• Inter-agency working

- Multiprofessional audit, emphasising clinical diagnosis
- Implementing the CPA, supported by patient-based registers, and improved resources for areas of particular need
- Clinical leadership

A protocol was developed for assessing services for people with severe mental illness, including schizophrenia and severe affective disorder (Wing et al 1995). The protocol was split into two parts assessing the purchasing and providing of mental health services. The purchasing section asked questions about:

1. Mental health needs assessment
2. Purchasing strategy
3. Commissioning and the interaction between purchasers and providers
4. The service specification and contract(s) for mental health services
5. Contract monitoring and the requirements for information
6. Implementation, quality and audit procedures
7. Interactions with other purchasers
8. General practitioner fundholding
9. Local authority social services

The providers section (of mental health services) asked questions about:

1. Community services
2. Rehabilitation and activity
3. Clinical interventions
4. Violence and self-harm
5. Crisis management
6. Short-stay hospital care
7. Secure longer-term hospital care
8. Longer term NHS (and NHS hostel) accommodation
9. Other (mostly non-NHS) accommodation
10. Clinical records
11. Local health service audit procedures
12. Education of mental health practitioners
13. Local community services
14. Primary care liaison
15. Social Services and local authority departments
16. Users, carers and voluntary organisations
17. Morale and leadership

The protocol used various rating scales to measure both provider and purchaser clinical standards:

- Scale A: how far services have taken action to ensure that individual guidelines have been met (0–9)
- Scale B: for rating overall quality (0–4)
- Scale C: measures accessibility of service (0–7)
- Scale D: identifies the organisation responsible for supplying or funding a service
- PAG Scale: optional means of checking the quality of residential accommodation (0–7)

The protocol provides a detailed overall assessment of the purchasing and provision of services for people with severe mental health problems. It may be used for statistical comparisons as long as key variables are taken into account (socio-economic factors, availability of resources, and recent organisational stability; Wing et al 1995). The use of the audit cycle would allow for a wide variety of local use intended to locate and rectify specific problems.

SERVICE EVALUATION

It has been proposed that service evaluation differs from research in a number of ways (Barker et al 1994). Service evaluation aims to assist decision making, rather than adding to an existing body of knowledge; it is completed to serve a person in a position of authority (a manager) often separate from the investigator; the evaluation is conducted in a non-controlled setting as opposed to the controlled research environment, and findings from the evaluation are often not translated for professional journals and are often used primarily at a local level.

More recently information gained through service evaluation is being published in professional journals (*Clinical Psychology Forum, British Journal of Psychiatry, Psychiatric Bulletin*) and more specialised journals (*Quality in Health Care, International Journal of Health Care and Quality Assurance, International Journal of Quality and Audit and Audit Trends*). This trend has brought about the national/international dissemination of information to professionals and consequently increased interest and awareness in audit-related issues.

Service evaluation approaches have been well reviewed in two books: *Research Methods in Clinical and Counselling Psychology* (Barker et al 1994) and *Quality and Excellence in Human Services* (Dickens 1994). Chris Barker and colleagues (1994) indicated that two questions needed to be addressed prior to implementing a process to evaluate services: "What is the service trying to do?" and "Why is the service trying to do that?" Paul Dickens (1994) went on to discuss the process for implementing an evaluation of a service. He raised five further questions that needed to be addressed: "Who wants the evaluation?" "What do they want from the evaluation?" "Why do they want the evaluation?" "When do they want the evaluation?" and "What resources are available for the evaluation?" He identified a four-stage process as follows:

1. Defining the program and its components, and setting the purpose of the evaluation
2. Developing an evaluation approach methodology
3. Carrying out the evaluation using the design and methods selected
4. Reporting the results

Various examples of mental health service evaluation have been published (Dutta et al 1991, Orrell & Johnson 1992, Parry 1992, Spear et al 1995). Some of the methods used to evaluate services are presented. The following examples represent various service evaluations of a number of mental health service areas. These include evaluations of a mental health service, two psychiatric units and three day centres. The examples were chosen to demonstrate a cross-sectional evaluation of the various mental health services.

The first example is a cross-sectional study of a community-orientated mental health service (Spear et al 1995). The aim of the evaluation was to carry out a survey of a general community-based mental health service to determine the case mix of patients in contact with the service, and to describe the services allocated to each individual in terms of the setting to which treatment was provided and the key workers' professional background. The study findings enabled the investigators to comment on which patients with specific psychiatric conditions were in contact with the services and the level of treatment/intervention each received. The authors indicate that the disadvantage of the cross-sectional evaluation is that it cannot assess change outcomes or the extent to which the service meets the needs of its target population.

A study comparing two acute psychiatric units using the St Helens and Knowsley audit schedule – a measure developed in local audit meetings – was completed (Dutta et al 1991). The study compared length of stay, how the patients were referred, the percentage of diagnosis, the use of ECT and the number of patients admitted on a section of the Mental Health Act (1983). The information gained from the study was used for comparison with previous study statistics to determine whether admission rates and length of stay were similar. The findings were used to action plan, after identifying that some form of crisis intervention would aid reduction in some short-term admissions. The outcome resulted in the establishment of a crisis intervention centre. It is important at this stage to stress the need to carry on through the audit process and review the imple- mented service intervention's effectiveness (introduction of the crisis intervention centre) to determine whether the number of short-term admissions was reduced as a result of the intervention. It is this stage that is often missing from audit studies, frequently termed the "closing the audit cycle".

The audit of three psychiatric day centres was used to compare the client population of each day centre to consider implications for service provision (Orrell & Johnson 1992). Clients' notes were examined and managers interviewed to obtain information for each attender on age, sex, support, housing, diagnosis, drug treatment, catchment area, original referral, duration and frequency of attend- ance, appropriateness of placement, date of last review and expected duration of attendance in future. The findings were used to decide whether resources were appropriately used in serving the needs of the psychiatric population.

Attempts to evaluate more specialised services have been completed. An important review article was published outlining approaches to improving psychotherapy services, its audit and evaluation (Parry 1992) using Maxwell's six-category framework (Maxwell 1984). Glenys Parry stated that "unmonitored practice is no longer defensible". Evaluation of specialised services like psychotherapy presents a number of problems depending on which theoretical model is used in practice. It was proposed that to audit psycho- therapy it is important to focus on the quality of the psychotherapy performed (Fonagy & Higgitt 1989). A model for developing clinical guidelines and audit of psychotherapy services has been developed and is discussed in more detail in Chapter 9 (Roth & Fonagy 1996).

PATIENT SATISFACTION QUESTIONNAIRES

The use of patient satisfaction questionnaires for audit purposes is considered important in the development of services based on the needs of the community which the organisation serves. Since the Griffiths (1983) report the health service has tried to develop a more consumer-driven service. The need to gain consumer feedback can be obtained by involving patients/clients in the planning of services (Jones et al 1987) and satisfaction questionnaires.

Fitzpatrick (1991) indicated that patient satisfaction is a valuable measure of health care, providing an important outcome measure. He highlighted its usefulness in assessing consultations and patterns of communication. If used systematically, feedback enables choice between alternatives in organising or providing health care. However, problems still remain concerning the development of measures to estimate patient satisfaction. Some key questions need to be addressed, namely: how should the information be collected (interview/self-report)? who should the information be collected from (patient, carer, professional)? and what are the key components that constitute patient satisfaction? These questions are addressed in the following discussion on patient satisfaction information collection.

Client satisfaction questionnaires are usually assessed by self-report measures or semi-structured interviews. Various measures of consumer satisfaction have been developed. Some examples of these include the Patient Satisfaction Questionnaire (PSQ; Ware et al 1983), the Parent Satisfaction Questionnaire (Stallard 1996; used in child services for parent interpretation of intervention), the Client Satisfaction Questionnaire – two versions CSQ-18 and CSQ-8 (Larsen et al 1979, Attkisson & Zwick 1982) – and the Hospital Patient Satisfaction Inventory (HPSI; Hardy et al 1996). One of the major problems with client satisfaction questionnaires is that they are often self-developed to meet the needs of the service area; difficulties then arise in terms of reliability of newly developed measures (Barker et al 1994). Estimating the reliability of satisfaction questionnaires can be difficult since satisfaction is thought to change over time and can be influenced by outcome (Stallard 1996). Consequently, variation in reported patient satisfaction may be associated with actual change in views than poor reliability (Fitzpatrick 1991, Bamford & Jacoby 1992).

Dickens (1994) identified a number of problems with methods of collecting information and subsequent results obtained from mental health studies into consumers' perception of services, quoting from a review completed by LeBow (1982). The main limitations associated with the studies were that they lacked information concerning the reliability of their methods; there were also practicality and validity problems.

The difficulty in obtaining information that is unbiased presents the evaluator with a number of challenges. When approaching patients following treatment the response is all too often a positive one (Weinstein 1979, Anderson 1991). The attainment of positive feedback is of course what service professionals and managers want; however, the nature of the positive feedback is often attributed to the "halo effect" (Anderson 1991). That is when the positive feedback is based on the patients' need to be grateful for what ever service they receive.

Not only positive results are obtained from patients when collecting information to estimate patient satisfaction with services and care provided. Negative results have been reported; however, it was only possible to identify problems with services by obtaining information in an indirect way. The findings were based mainly on the patients' actions rather than through interview of complaint (Stiles et al 1979, Baker & Whitfield 1992).

Riordan & Mockler (1996), using a three-way interpretation of services provided and outcomes (patient, carer/next of kin, and key worker) reported closer agreement between patient and carer than service key worker following interview. The key worker often over-estimated the quality of care provided and outcomes. The patients and carers were found to be more comfortable with disclosing dissatisfaction with services provided when interviewed at home following discharge and when it was pointed out that they would not be identified by name.

Fitzpatrick (1991) identified the advantages of self-completed versus interview questionnaires. He indicated that the use of interview provides sensitivity to patients' concerns and flexibility in covering topics, establishes a rapport, clarifies ambiguities of items or of reasons for views, and provides respondent adherence and more scope to follow up non-respondents. The use of self-completed questionnaires provides standardisation of items, no interviewer bias, anonymity, low cost of data gathering and less need for staff training. On the negative side, interviews can be very time consuming and self-report postal responses often have a low level of compliance. Negative assumptions about surveys of patient satisfaction are often made (Fitzpatrick 1991). These include the uncovering of widespread and general dissatisfaction with services, and the finding that patients' answers are often ill considered or whimsical and that misjudgements can be made arising from patients' reliance on perceptions based on surrogate indicators (halo effect).

Hardy and colleagues (1996) using information from two separate hospital groups of 700 and 483 patients (using self-completed questionnaires) and factor analysis identified three main components of proximal patient satisfaction. The three areas were satisfaction with the quality of care provided by nurses, doctors and managers and the general ambience of the hospital; knowledge of and improvement in health; and the psychology of hospitalisation, including items concerned with anxiety, loneliness and lack of control over what happens in hospital. Furthermore, they identified three aspects of care that best predicted satisfaction: namely nursing and medical representatives' information practices, socialisation procedures (patients' initial encounter with the hospital, the attitudes of reception staff, the explanation of ward routines and introductions of staff) and patient participation in the care process.

Three studies of patient satisfaction identified a number of dimensions associated with patient satisfaction (Fitzpatrick 1991, Riordan & Mockler 1994, Hardy et al 1996). Some of the common components identified in Table 1 when comparing study findings include overall quality satisfaction of care delivery and outcome, access to services, the provision of information, staff–patient interaction (and staff attitudes) and the patients' general comfort. These may be used to provide useful indicators of dimensions to be considered when developing patient satisfaction questionnaires.

Table 1 Dimensions of patient satisfaction

Fitzpatrick (1991)

Humanness	Cost
Informativeness	Facilities
Overall quality	Outcome
Competence	Continuity
Bureaucracy	Attention to psychosocial problems
Access	

Riordan & Mockler (1994)

Staff–patient relations	Access to services
Provision of information	Response/waiting times
General comfort	Overall outcome
Patient carer involvement in care process	

Hardy et al (1996)

Overall satisfaction	Comfort
Arrival at hospital and first impressions	General care
Nursing and medical care provided	Health
(information provided, staff attitudes)	General feelings
Other staff attitudes	

Chapter 8

METHODS OF AUDIT DATA ANALYSIS

Statistical methods of analysis are formal techniques which assist in the interpretation of audit data. Crombie and colleagues (1993) indicated that the needs for use of statistical methods in audit are few and straightforward, and are usually needed to help answer three types of question: (1) is care satisfactory? (2) what are the possible reasons for this? and (3) was the intervention followed by change? However, more complex statistics are increasingly becoming a feature of audit as it moves towards the analysis of treatment outcome, patient satisfaction, clinical effectiveness, service evaluation and the development of measurement tools for audit purposes. The following provides a discussion about how various forms of data analysis may be used for audit purposes, using examples of methods used in published audit studies. It is not an exhaustive account of methods of analysis used for audit, and many other approaches may be used in practice. Each method listed will be discussed individually.

- Descriptive statistics
- Inferential statistical evaluation
  (Parametric/non-parametric)
  - Tests of difference
  - Tests of correlation
  - Trend analysis
- Spot checks (on data, records, practice)
  using pre-defined standards and criteria
- Goal achievement and problem resolution

DESCRIPTIVE STATISTICS

This form of data interpretation is by far the most commonly used approach for audit purposes (Firth-Cozens 1993). One of the most complete audit studies in mental health used only descriptive statistics to interpret their data (Pippard 1992b). It is often useful to translate raw data gained from audit into a more understandable form for presentation. The following is a description of some of the more popular methods of descriptive data analysis, interpretation and presentation in the audit literature.

Raw Scores

Raw scores are the most basic form of data. These are often large amounts of numbers with no sensible meaning in their current form. By eyeballing small amounts of data it is often easy to identify distinct differences between two sets of information without having to complete any form of statistical analysis. However, larger amounts of data would require some form of statistical interpretation.

Measures of Central Tendency

When analysing raw data it is often useful to calculate the average of the scores. This can be measured in three different ways using the mean, median and mode.

Mean

The mean is the arithmetic average. It is calculated by adding up all the scores and dividing the result by the number of scores, e.g. 4, 6, 1, 3, 5, 4, 6, 2 = 31, divided by 8 = 3.9.

Advantages of Using the Mean

- The mean is the most sensitive of the estimates of central tendency covered in this section.
- It accounts for the total and individual values of all scores
- It is the statistic used in estimating population parameters. This estimation is the basis for the highly sensitive parametric tests (discussed in inferential statistics section), used to show significant differences between mean estimates. (Note: population parameters are measures taken from all of a target group (e.g. all of the female population of the UK). The mean is used to make estimates of population parameters from a sample taken from that population.)

Disadvantages of Using the Mean

- It is less sensitive in detecting a small number of high scores (causing an inflated mean estimate) in a larger number of small scores. The median is more sensitive in detecting the discrepancy in a large set of scores.
- It is laborious to calculate if using large sets of numbers

Median

The median is the middle score of a group of scores, the central value of a set of numbers. When using the median it is important to be aware that some information is lost in the calculation process. However, when using skewed data (when the mean, median and mode have different values; see Frequency Distributions, below) the mean is most affected and the median gives a truer estimate of central tendency. It is found by placing the scores in order of size and finding the middle number, e.g. 2, 5, 7, 10, 11, 15, 21, 28 = 10.5.

Advantages of Using the Median

- The median is more representative when extreme values in one direction are present in the data set.
- It is obtainable even when extreme values are unknown.
- It is easier to calculate than the mean.

Disadvantages of Using the Median

- The median cannot be used in the estimation of population parameters.
- If using only a small amount of numbers the calculation may not be truly representative.
- It extracts less information than the mean because it does not account for exact values of each number.

Mode

The mode is the score that occurs most frequently. It accounts for only the frequency of occurrence of different values and does not involve any form of calculation on the numbers. It is most useful where no further information about the data is available. It is found by simply viewing the data and identifying the most commonly occurring number, e.g. 3, 7, 5, 6, 7, 3, 8, 7 = 7.

Advantages of Using the Mode

- The mode is not affected by extreme values going in one direction.
- It is easy to find and does not require any calculation.
- It identifies the important value of a number set.
- It is obtainable even when extreme values are unknown.

Disadvantages of Using the Mode

- It cannot be used in the estimation of population parameters.
- It is a crude estimate, especially when using small amounts of numbers where there are possibly several modes.
- It does not account for exact values of each number.

Ranked Scores

Ranked scores show the relationship between scores. You can determine who has the highest/lowest score. It can be used to show total or individual order of differences between wards/units on a number of measures.

Ward	PSQ mean scores (for 60 patients for each ward)	Ranked score
1	35	3
2	30	2
3	55	4.5
4	22	1
5	55	4.5
6	60	6

If two rank scores are the same then the ranking is shared. The ranks work in reverse order to the normal representation of number one allocated to the ward with the highest level of patient satisfaction.

Measures of dispersion

The mean does not always show the spread of scores when comparing two groups if the numbers in one group are more spread out than numbers in the other group but both groups have the same mean. Consequently, some other measure is required to show the difference.

Range

The range is calculated by subtracting the bottom value of a data set from the top value of the same data set and then adding 1. The 1 allows for possible measurement error.

For example, the number of patients treated in eight different departments from two mental health units:

Unit 1 10, 15, 21, 35, 40, 43, 60, 85 = 85 − 10 = 75 + 1: the range is 76
Unit 2 55, 64, 89, 91, 97, 105, 108, 114 = 114 − 55 = 59 + 1: the range is 60

Semi-interquartile Range

This statistic concentrates on the distance between the two values which cut off the bottom and top 25% of scores. The two values are known as the 25th and 75th percentiles respectively. The semi-interquartile range is half of the distance between the two percentile values (25th and 75th). The calculation of the semi-interquartile range means that the estimate will not be affected by any central grouping of values (unlike the standard range calculation). The semi-interquartile range is calculated by finding the 1st (Q1) and 3rd quartile (Q2) (the 25th and 75th percentile respectively). This is achieved by identifying the median value (which is the 2nd quartile and also the 50th percentile) and then moving one quartile to the left (to find the 1st quartile) and one quartile to the right (to find the 3rd quartile) of the median. Then subtract Q1 from Q2 and divide by 2.

For example, the number of admissions to nine wards over a six-month period:

10, 15, 21, 35, 40, 43, 55, 60, 85 = 21 (Q1) − 55 (Q2) = 34, divided by 2: the semi-interquartile range is 17

Mean Deviation

A deviation value is the difference between any particular value and the mean. It is a measure of how far that value deviates from the mean. The range and semi-interquartile take no notice and some notice respectively of the way values deviate from the mean. To calculate the mean deviation you must first identify the mean, subtract the mean from each value to obtain a set of deviations, add up all these deviations (take no notice of minus signs) and then divide by the result of the last step by the number of values.

For example (using patient satisfaction scores from seven patients):

Score		Mean		Deviation
4	–	3.9	=	0.1
6	–	3.9	=	2.1
1	–	3.9	=	–2.9
3	–	3.9	=	–0.9
5	–	3.9	=	1.1
4	–	3.9	=	0.1
6	–	3.9	=	2.1

Deviation total = 9.3, divided by number of values ($N=7$):
mean deviation = 1.3

Standard Deviation

The standard deviation (SD) measures the distribution of scores around the mean. If the SD of a group of scores is large, this means that the scores are widely distributed, with many scores occurring a long way from the mean. If the SD is small, most scores occur close to the mean. The lowest SD is zero, indicating that there is no difference in scores.

If the scores are normally distributed (see Frequency Distributions, below), a knowledge of the SD informs the investigator what proportion of scores falls within certain limits. 68.3% of all scores lie between +1 and –1 SD from the mean (1 SD above and below the mean). 95.4% of all scores lie between +2 and –2 SD from the mean.

For example:

Score		Mean		Deviation	Squared deviation
4	–	3.9	=	0.1	0.01
6	–	3.9	=	2.1	4.41
1	–	3.9	=	–2.9	8.41
3	–	3.9	=	–0.9	0.81
5	–	3.9	=	1.1	1.21
4	–	3.9	=	0.1	0.01
6	–	3.9	=	2.1	4.41

Sum of squared deviations = 19.3, divided by the number of values ($N=7$) = 2.75 (this figure is the variance)
Square root of 2.75 = 1.66 (the standard deviation)

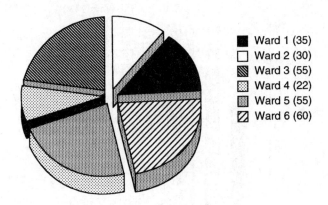

Ward 1 (35)
Ward 2 (30)
Ward 3 (55)
Ward 4 (22)
Ward 5 (55)
Ward 6 (60)

Figure 1   Mean Patient Satisfaction Questionnaire Scores for Each Ward

Graphs/Bar Charts/Pie Charts

The use of visual representation to demonstrate information gained from audit is important in report writing and for presentations using overhead projectors. The information can be more easily digested using various methods of visual presentation. The availability of various graphic software packages aids the process of preparing data for presentation.

Pie Charts

The pie chart is a circular shape divided into sections demonstrating how much is attributed to each area (part) that makes up the whole. The chart can demonstrate mean score (see Figure 1), percentages of raw scores estimates. The chart can be divided into broken or attached segments and can be displayed in three dimensions or normal presentation depending on what software computer package is used. The pie chart used in the example was completed using Ami-Pro for Windows, 3.1 version. It is evident from the chart that ward 6 has the highest level of patient satisfaction, closely followed by wards 5 and 3. Ward 4 has the lowest level of patient satisfaction (see Figure 1).

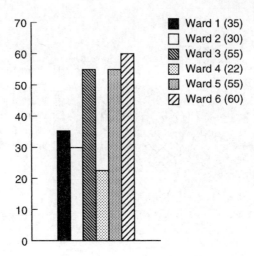

Figure 2   Mean Patient Satisfaction Questionnaire Scores for Each Ward

Bar Charts

The bar chart is a popular method of displaying mean scores or raw data. The method is a far better approach to presenting data compared with a tabled depiction of information. The chart consists of y- and x-axes. The vertical axis is the y-axis and would normally show the dependent variable (in this case scores from the PSQ in Figure 2). The x-axis demonstrates the independent variables (the six wards). It is important to ensure that the chart is clearly labelled and easy to understand. The chart was completed using Ami-Pro for Windows, 3.1 version.

Line Graph

The line graph is more limited in its use compared with bar charts, pie charts and other forms of data presentation. The dependent variable is generally displayed on the y-axis (vertical axis).

The line graph displayed in the example (Figure 3) shows the mean number of CPA meetings for a community mental health team. The mean scores of each month are plotted for the 12 months of the year. The data is presented on the y-axis and the x-axis. This method of presentation is optional: the data can be presented in various ways. The data used shows a gradual increase in CPA meetings convened,

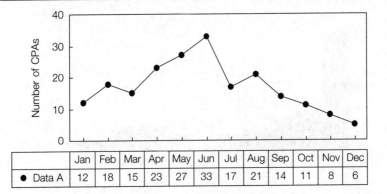

	Jan	Feb	Mar	Apr	May	Jun	Jul	Aug	Sep	Oct	Nov	Dec
● Data A	12	18	15	23	27	33	17	21	14	11	8	6

Figure 3 Mean Number of CPA Meetings for a Community Mental Health Team

peaking in the summer months and decreasing in the autumn and winter months. Because the data is linked by the graph it makes it easier to identify trends in meeting activities. The graph was completed using Lotus 1-2-3 release 5 for Windows computer software package.

Histograms

The total area within the histogram is equal to the sample size number of scores. Its main characteristics are that all categories are represented, the columns are equal width per equal category interval and all intervals are represented even if empty.

The example in Figure 4 shows the number of patients ($N=150$) that waited to see their therapist between 5 and 30 minutes after their given appointment time in outpatients across a mental health unit over a one-year period. The chart shows that the majority of delays lasted for between 5 and 15 minutes. The number of patients experiencing delay evens out between 20 and 30 minutes. When presented in this form it is easier for therapists and other mental health workers to see the extent of any problems that exist. The figure also shows the standard deviation, mean and total number of patients used in the representation. The graph was completed using the graphics package in SPSS for Windows, version 6.1.3. Not all graphics packages may have this option.

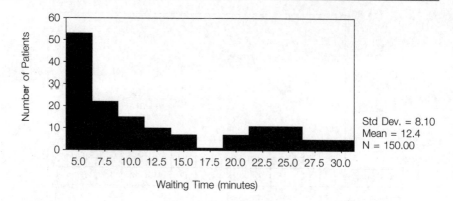

Figure 4   Time Spent by Patients Waiting to See Therapists in Outpatients

Scattergram (Scatter Diagram or Scatterplot)

The scattergram is useful for graphically demonstrating an association between two variables showing the scattering of pairs. Each point represents one person's score on the two variables (non-compliance to medication and hospital readmissions). The scattergram is a useful diagram to use if you suspect an association between two variables prior to using more inferential methods such as correlational analysis (see tests of correlation: Spearman's Rho and Pearson's Product–Moment tests, below) to obtain a level of statistical significance.

The example scattergram (Figure 5) demonstrates a positive association between medication non-compliance and hospital readmissions. The diagram shows the points clustered closely together moving in a diagonal direction from the zero point joining the *x*- and *y*-axes to the highest points of the axes, with the number of readmissions increasing with the incidence of non-compliance to medication. The negative association would be demonstrated by a diagonal line running from the top end of the *y*-axis to the top end of the *x*-axis. A zero correlation would be represented as a spread of points distributed unevenly about the graph with no clear line direction. Figures 6–8 show what positive, negative and zero correlations respectively would look like if lines were drawn through the cluster of points. The scattergram (Figure 5) was completed using the graphics package in SPSS for Windows, version 6.1.3.

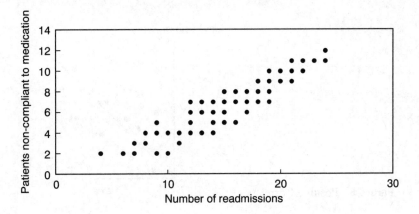

Figure 5 The Relationship Between Non-compliance to Medication and Readmissions

FREQUENCY DISTRIBUTIONS

Normal Distribution (Mean, Median and Mode occur at the same value)

The normal distribution is found when the data used is continuous, that is, each score is the result of a number of randomly distributed effects causing the score to increase or decrease and when a large number of scores drawn randomly from a population are used.

Skewed Distribution (Mean, Median and Mode have different values)

The skewed distribution often occurs when a small sample is used, or when a biased sample is taken from a normally distributed population and when a measuring scale has an attainable cut-off point.

INFERENTIAL STATISTICS

Statistics test hypotheses (ideas) about the effect of certain variables on others. There are two main types of hypothesis: the experimental

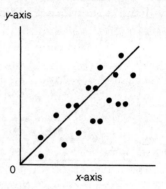

Figure 6   Positive Correlation

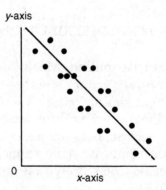

Figure 7   Negative Correlation

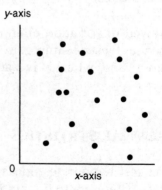

Figure 8   No Correlation

and null hypothesis. The experimental hypothesis proposes that there will be a significant difference between conditions. The null hypothesis states that there will be no significant difference between conditions. If the outcome of the study does not show a difference between the two conditions then the null hypothesis is accepted and the experimental hypothesis is rejected.

The manipulation of variables is used to demonstrate whether there is a predicted relationship between two variables. The most common method of achieving this is by manipulating one of the variables to see whether it has an effect on the other variable. The variable which is manipulated is known as the independent variable. The dependent variable is influenced by the manipulation of the independent variable. It is important to control other variables (extraneous variables) other than the independent variable to ensure they do not affect the outcome. Uncontrolled extraneous variables are known as confounding variables.

For example, measuring clinical outcomes following treatment may be achieved by comparing the effects of symptom change (dependent variable) with the type of therapy/treatment used (independent variable). An example of an extraneous variable would be if the patient was receiving another form of treatment (e.g. medication) with the therapy intervention being rated for its effectiveness on symptom change. To control for the extraneous variables the investigator may use three groups: (1) patients receiving psychotherapy only (independent variable 1); (2) patients receiving medication only (independent variable 2); and (3) patients receiving no treatment (independent variable 3). The measure of symptom change pre/post treatment would be the dependent variable. If a patient's symptom change was estimated without controlling for various treatment interventions these would be confounding variables.

In most experiments it is not clear whether the result achieved occurred due to manipulation of the independent variable or because of chance variables. Statistical tests give the probability that the result occurred due to chance. The most common level of significance (i.e., the result is unlikely to have occurred by chance and is likely to be repeatable) is 0.05 or smaller. If greater than 0.05 the outcome is said to be not significant.

Since significance is a matter of probability rather than certainty errors can be made in assuming that a significant difference was due to the effects of manipulating an independent variable or non-significant result due to chance factors. These errors are known as type 1 and type 2 errors:

T1 Result is significant but it turns out to be an unreliable result
T2 Result is not significant but it turns out to be genuine.

TYPES OF DATA

Data comes in a variety of different types and it is very important from the point of view of analysis to know what type of data you have.

Nominal Data

Nominal data does not scale items on a dimension, but rather labels them. When simply counting the number of subjects that fall into one category or another you are using nominal or frequency data; for example, how many patients were admitted to various wards over a six-month period and what their diagnoses were gives two categories of nominal data: ward and diagnoses.

Ordinal Data

This type of data does indicate the position of a score in a group. It orders objects, events and people along some continuum. It does not tell you the level of difference between the ranking positions, e.g. which ward had the most/least admissions over a given period of time.

Interval/Ratio Data

Interval and ratio data do more than just order the data: they show differences between the data. The measures used in estimates of symptom change are examples of interval data, e.g. when a 1 point

Table 1

Subjects *Same (S)/Different (D)*	Design	Description
(S) Repeated measures (also within groups or between conditions)	Related	Each subject performs in both conditions
(D) Matched pairs	Related	Subjects are sorted into matched pairs (matching age, sex, abilities, etc.). Then one from each pair performs in groups 1 and 2
(D) Independent subjects (also independent samples, between groups or independent groups)	Unrelated	Each subject performs in different conditions

difference means the same along any point of the scale. These two types of data differ in only one respect: ratio data has a logical zero point whereas zero on an interval scale is a purely arbitrary point.

RESEARCH DESIGN (see Table 1)

Repeated measures and matched pairs are two of the related designs. They are related because a value in one condition is directly related to a value in another condition and therefore both can be directly compared using statistical methods.

The independent designs belong to a category known as unrelated designs (i.e., independent subject/group designs). In this approach a completely different set of subjects are measured on each condition and consequently the outcome scores are unrelated.

STATISTICAL TESTS USED FOR AUDIT DATA ANALYSIS

The following is a basic description of some of the statistical tests that can be used for data analysis (see Figure 9). The tests described are not an exhaustive list of the tests available. Factorial analysis of variance, multiple regression, analysis of covariance and log–linear analysis are not discussed in this chapter. The purpose is to provide

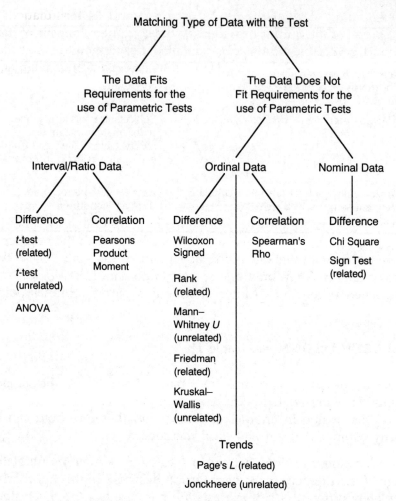

Figure 9 Decision Tree for Choosing a Test

a basic understanding of some of the tests that are available and that may be used for statistical analysis of audit data. Each test will be detailed using actual examples of analysis using audit data (where possible) to facilitate understanding. The discussion does not provide the formulae for each test. Most of the data analysis described can be completed using computer software packages which complete the data analysis for the investigator (SPSS, Minitab, EXECUSTAT, EcStatic, BMDP, JMP, SAS, CSS). However, it is important for the person completing the data analysis to have an understanding of what the test is used for (and its formulation) to make sense of the output provided by the computer analysis of data. A list of books providing more detailed descriptions of statistical analysis and test formulae is provided at the end of this chapter.

Non-Parametric Statistics

Tests of Difference

Chi Square

This test is used on nominal data and is based on the allocation of subjects into categories. The test compares the number of subjects/ observations in each category and compares this with the number of observations which would be expected if there was no relationship between the variables.

For example, chi square was used to measure the effectiveness of a discharge co-ordinator to improve the quality of hospital discharge. The study evaluated the effectiveness of discharge by counting the number of readmissions, the number of problems after discharge and the receipt of services (Houghton et al 1996). The test was also used to determine whether the introduction of a protocol for ECT practice (stimulus alteration and requirement for restimulation) – developed following audit of current practice – improved the administration of ECT (Robertson et al 1995). The Yates correction was used in this study. The Yates correction for continuity (Yates 1934) is often used with chi square when the study produces a small sample or if using finite sample sizes.

Sign Test

The sign test is used for repeated measures (or matched pairs) on the same categories, again using nominal data. The test is a basic test of difference that simply counts the number of times one condition is larger than the other and compares this with what would be expected by chance if there was no real difference between the conditions.

For example, in investigating the number of complaints all wards received in a mental health unit at one year – prior to the intro-

duction of an action plan to improve staff/patient/relative interaction – and at two years following the introduction of the action
plan, the test would count differences in the number of complaints
(pre/post action plan) for each ward.

Wilcoxon Signed Rank Test

This test investigates ordinal data using a two-condition related
design when the same subjects perform under both conditions. It
examines the differences between the subjects' scores in each
condition. It looks at the direction of difference and the relative size
of those differences by ranking them in the same way as described
in the Ranked Scores section under Descriptive Statistics.

For example, the test may be used when comparing a number of
community mental health teams' score ratings of adherence to pre-
defined standards, using audit criteria to rate standard compliance
(pre and post introduction). The test would estimate whether the
introduction of the standards resulted in statistically significant
changes in practice.

Mann–Whitney U

The Mann–Whitney U is used to compare two different groups of
subjects using ordinal data. The test compares the size of scores in
both conditions for difference. If most of the large scores are in one
condition, this reduces the likelihood that the difference between the
two conditions was due to chance alone.

For example, the test was used to investigate audit activity and the
quality of completed audit projects in primary care (Chambers et al
1995). The study attempted to identify associations between the
characteristics of primary health care practices and quality criteria of
audit practices (choice of topic, staff participation, setting standards,
methods of data collection, presentation of results, plan and make
changes, whether plan led to set standards being achieved). The
Mann–Whitney U test was used when two levels of the characteristic were compared (e.g. whether the practice manager was
present or absent).

Friedman

The Friedman test is used for related designs when the same (or matched) subjects are performing under three or more conditions. It is an extension of the Wilcoxon test. It rank orders the scores for each subject and then compares the totals of ranks for each condition.

An example would be the investigation of primary carers' (caring for relatives with dementia in the community) satisfaction with care provision, with the community mental health team using a newly implemented CPA case review system. The test may be used to compare carers' satisfaction rating scores at four, eight and 12 months.

Kruskal–Wallis Test

The Kruskal–Wallis test is used for unrelated designs when different subjects perform under three or more conditions. It compares the ranked total of scores for each condition for differences using the same method as the Mann–Whitney U.

For example, the test was used to compare differences in patients' rating satisfaction of care provided between a number of hospitals and wards (Thomas et al 1996).

Correlation

In some studies it may be useful to investigate the relationship between two sets of variables, e.g. hospital admissions and non-compliance with medication. There are three possible outcomes for this form of analysis:

1. A positive correlation (hospital admissions vary directly with non-compliance with medication)
2. A negative correlation (hospital admissions vary inversely with non-compliance with medication)
3. No correlation (no relationship exists between admissions and non-compliance)

Correlations or associations between two variables lie on a continuum with zero in the middle (no correlation) and −1 and +1 at each end of the scale (−1 or +1 = perfect correlation). The closer the correlation coefficient is to zero, the lower is the level of association. The closer the correlation is to +1 or −1, the more significant is the association. However, the difference between 0.1 and 0.9 is very great. The scale does not have regular intervals between each coefficient. Therefore, 0.1 and 0.2 are a lot closer to a zero correlation than 0.8 and 0.9 to a perfect correlation. This point is demonstrated in the following diagram:

◄──────────── Increasing degree of association ────────────►
−1 −0.9 −0.8 −0.7 −0.6 −0.5 −0.4 −0.3 −0.2 −0.1 0 0.1 0.2 0.3 0.4 0.5 0.6 0.7 0.8 0.9 +1

A common mistake is to assume that because two variables correlate, one causes the other. Correlation does not imply causation. There are two tests of the statistical significance of an association between two variables, namely Spearman's rho and Pearson's product–moment tests. Spearman's rho will be discussed next; see Parametric Statistics: Correlation, below, for a discussion of Pearson's test.

Spearman's Rho

Spearman's rho measures the amount and significance of a correlation between subjects' scores on two variables. It can be used for most forms of data (with the exception of nominal data). It is mainly used when the data does not fit the requirements for the use of parametric tests.

For example, the test was used in the investigation into the attitudes of general practitioners to audit. The investigators tested for associations between statement responses, i.e. attitudes to audit and the general practitioners' personal characteristics (practices, experience of audit, sex and number of years qualified) (Chambers et al 1996).

Trend Analysis

Often investigators will predict a trend between various sets of variables. It is sometimes a useful exercise to demonstrate whether the trend exists. This can be achieved using inferential statistical methods if large quantities of data have been collected and if the investigator wants to know if the trend is statistically significant. The use of trend analysis tests would be preferable in these cases to the tests of difference described in this section of the chapter. If small amounts of data have been collected then the investigator may choose to use only descriptive statistics to interpret the data and demonstrate the trend.

Page's L Trend Test

Page's L trend test can be used to investigate trends between three or more conditions. The test should be used for a related design (i.e., when the same or matched subjects have completed all conditions). The test is an extension of the Friedman test. It ranks the data and the investigator predicts whether the rank totals will fall in a certain order. In trend tests it is standard practice to arrange the conditions in the predicted order, with lowest scores on the left and highest scores on the right (based on the investigator's trend prediction). This rule also applies to the Jonckheere test discussed next.

For example, the test may be used to identify trends in the involvement of patients in the planning of their care. A group of patients served by a community mental health team would rate their perceived level of involvement in the care planning process at two, four and six months (following the introduction of guidelines concerning the involvement of patients in care planning). The investigator would be able to identify whether a statistically significant trend was evident, i.e. gradual increase in involvement, decrease or no change.

Jonckheere Trend Test

The Jonckheere trend test can be used to investigate trends between three or more conditions. The test should be used for unrelated designs (e.g. when different subjects perform under different conditions). The test is an extension of the Kruskal–Wallis test. It counts the number of scores which are higher in each condition than scores in previous conditions. If there are only chance differences the scores in each condition should be roughly equal. It is essential when using the Jonckheere test to have equal numbers of subjects under each condition.

For example, the test may be used to evaluate readmission trends and their level of support in patients served by three different community mental health teams (CMHTs). Each CMHT would serve a similar type of population and have a comparable case mix. The investigator would identify the first 30 readmissions for each CMHT and then rate the level of support provided by the CMHT and supporting services. The analysis would determine whether there was a trend in the level of support provided by the three CMHTs and the number of readmissions.

Parametric Statistics

To use parametric tests the data needs to fit three requirements:

1. Data scores are drawn from a normally distributed population of scores.
2. The experimental scores are measured on an interval scale (ratio data can also be used).
3. The variability or range of scores for each condition should be roughly the same (homogeneity of variance).

If these requirements are not satisfied then the investigator should consider using the non-parametric equivalents of the parametric tests.

Tests of Difference

t-test (unrelated)

The t-test (unrelated) concerns interval/ratio data, with two conditions testing one independent variable, when different subjects are satisfying the two conditions (e.g. patient and their carer completing PSQs). The test compares the means of scores for both conditions, taking into account the variation of scores in the two conditions.

For example, the test was used to estimate clinical outcome and patient satisfaction between two groups (patients receiving home-based community care and standard inpatient followed by out-patient care). The study attempted to evaluate home-based versus community-based care for people with severe mental illness. The investigators anticipated that superior outcome is achieved using community care for severely mentally ill patients (Marks et al 1994).

t-*test (related)*

The *t*-test (related) concerns interval/ratio data, with two conditions testing one independent variable, when the same or matched subjects are satisfying both conditions. It compares the size of the difference between each subject's scores under the two conditions. It calculates the possibility of the size of the difference being due to chance accounting for the mean of the whole group and individual subject scores.

For example, a *t*-test was used to assess change in various dimensions of health status (mental health, social function, etc.) using the SF-36 General Health Questionnaire pre and post treatment (Dawson et al 1996).

Analysis of Variance (ANOVA)

ANOVA analyses several conditions, testing the effects of two or more independent variables. The aim is to break down the variance due to independent variables into the variance due to each variable separately and any interactions between these variables.

For example, the test was used to detect differences between four patient groups (first, previous, voluntary and detained admissions) for various illness characteristics (personal functioning, violence, anxiety/depression, positive/negative symptoms, overactivity, etc.), testing each characteristic across the four groups (i.e., a one-way ANOVA) (Lelliott et al 1994). A second example is the use of the test to demonstrate substantial differences in the prevalence of "new long-stay patients" when comparing UK countries (England, Northern Ireland, Scotland and Wales) (Lelliott & Wing 1994).

It is often useful to make comparisons between variables following ANOVA to identify more detailed levels of significance. Two comparisons can be made *a priori* (chosen before the data is collected) and *post hoc* (planned after the data is collected and a mean difference is known). Various tests of *a priori* (multiple *t*-tests; Dunn's test and/or Bonferroni *t*, 1961; linear contrasts, orthogonal contrasts) and *post hoc* (Newman–Keuls; Fisher's least significant difference procedure; Dunnett's test, 1955; Turkey's HSD (honestly significant difference) and WSD (wholly significant difference), 1949, 1953, 1977; Scheffe's test, 1953, 1959) comparisons exist. However, there are too many to discuss in any significant detail in this chapter (refer to statistical literature noted at the end of this chapter for further reading).

Correlation

See notes on non-parametric correlations, above, for general test details.

Pearson's Product–Moment Coefficient

This measures the amount and significance of a correlation between subjects' scores on two variables. The test is used when interval ratio data has been collected and when the data fits the requirements for use as a parametric test.

For example the test was used to identify a positive association between patient satisfaction and resolution of identified problems and a negative association between waiting times and patient satisfaction with care provision (Bucknall 1994).

SPOT CHECKS USING PRE-DEFINED STANDARDS AND CRITERIA

The use of spot checking areas of practice against pre-defined criteria and standards is a useful method of providing a snapshot of the current status of the service. It may involve analysis of data provided from one-day census of waiting times, visiting times (home visits), record keeping, carrying out treatment (lithium therapy, ECT). Spot checks can be pre-arranged or spontaneous. If pre-arranged the staff can take steps to ensure criteria are fulfilled and standards achieved. The more spontaneous visit can guard against these preparatory interventions.

The analysis of the information gained from spot checking can be completed by providing a rating scale for the criteria to measure against. The total could be used to provide an estimate of where a service is on a standard rating scale:

- *Criteria*: Outpatients seen by members of a CMHT were seen within 5 minutes of their given appointment time (5 minutes either side); 75 out of 100 patients were seen within 5 minutes of the stated appointment time (=75%).
- *Standard*: In 80% of cases outpatients will be seen by CMHT members within 5 minutes of their given appointment time.

It is evident from this example that the CMHT have not achieved their standard target for keeping appointment times. This information is useful to provide feedback information to the team and can be achieved using simple descriptive statistics. However, it does not provide the reasons why team members did not see their patients on time. This information is important to allow the team to identify problem areas and then plan changes to be able to achieve the standard. It is also useful to present a standard scale. If the feedback is that the team have not reached the required standard this can induce a feeling of total failure when in actual fact the team falls short of the standard by 5%. A standard scale shows where they are on a continuum of achieving the standard to not achieving the standard.

For example:

Standard	%
Achieved	80–100
Majority achieved	60–79
Half achieved	40–59
Partially achieved	20–39
Low level of achievement	01–19

The investigator could use inferential statistical estimates of change if following up the waiting times for appointments by checking the frequency of on-time/late appointment time from the first spot check to the follow-up check. The analysis could be completed using chi square to identify whether change in practice has reached statistical significance. Alternatively, the investigator could use purely descriptive methods of analysis as described above.

ACHIEVEMENT OF PRE-DEFINED OUTCOME GOALS AGAINST IDENTIFIED PROBLEMS

The analysis of outcome goals is normally achieved by identifying a patient's needs/problems and then setting a number of goals in attempting to resolve the problem or respond to unmet needs. The goals would be set pre treatment and then reassessed post intervention and, for thoroughness, by follow-up either six months or a year later.

The information may be analysed and presented case by case, not requiring any complex statistical analysis. This method provides the team involved in setting the goals with a body of detailed information to review clinical intervention and practice. However, some teams may also want feedback about the overall level of achieving outcome goals and problem resolution. This could be achieved by collecting information over a set period of time and then analysing the outcome goal data using inferential statistical analysis of change, comparing the severity of the patient's problems (using a rating scale) pre treatment with post-treatment estimates of the patient's problems. Depending on the type of data (see Figure 9) a statistical test may be chosen and used to provide feedback on the statistical significance of goal attainment by the measure of the severity of problems pre and post treatment.

The methods of data analysis described in this chapter may be used to evaluate various forms of data obtained from audit. The developing relationship between audit and research (discussed in more detail in Chapter 9) suggests the need for the use of more advanced methods of data analysis. Consequently, it is important for audit facilitators to be familiar with at least basic statistical methods of analysing data.

RECOMMENDED FURTHER READING

Introduction to Statistics

Coolican, H. (1990). *Research Methods and Statistics in Psychology*. London: Hodder & Stoughton.
Greene, J. & D'Oliveira, D. (1982). *Learning to Use Statistical Tests in Psychology*. Milton Keynes: Open University Press.

Heyes, S., Hardy, M., Humphreys, P. & Rookes, P. (1986). *Starting Statistics in Psychology and Education*. London: Weidenfeld & Nicolson.
Rowntree, D. (1991). *Statistics Without Tears: A Primer for Non-mathematicians*. London: Penguin.

More Advanced Statistics

Howell, D.C. (1992). *Statistical Methods for Psychology* (3rd edn). Belmont: Duxbury Press.
Leach, C. (1979). *Introduction to Statistics: A Nonparametric Approach for the Social Sciences*. New York: McGraw-Hill.
Siegal, S. & Castellan, N.J. (1988). *Nonparametric statistics* (2nd edn). New York: McGraw-Hill.
Tabachnick, B.G. & Fidell, L.S. (1983). *Using Multivariate Statistics*. London: Harper & Rowe.
Woodward, M. & Francis, L.M.A. (1988). *Statistics for Health Management and Research*. London: Arnold.

Using SPSS Computer Software packages

Foster, J.J. (1993). *Starting SPSS/PC+ and SPSS for Windows: A Beginner's Guide to Data Analysis* (2nd edn). Wilmslow: Sigma Press.
Kinnear, P.R. & Gray, C.D. (1994). *SPSS for Windows Made Simple*. Hove: Erlbaum.

Chapter 9

FUTURE DEVELOPMENTS

In this concluding chapter a number of issues related to the future of audit in the UK will be discussed. Likely developments which may increase the impact of audit include the *clinical effectiveness* initiative, the introduction of *clinical practice guidelines*, the development of *clinical informatics*, and the increasing emphasis on *service user* and *purchaser* involvement in audit.

AUDIT OR POOR RESEARCH: MEASURING CLINICAL EFFECTIVENESS

The relationship between audit and research has been an issue for debate since the introduction of audit in 1989 (Edwards 1991, Black 1992, Firth-Cozens & Ennis 1995, Paxton 1995, Firth-Cozens 1996, Roth & Fonagy 1996). Audit might be defined as the comparison of performance against agreed standards which must be set by high-quality research. It involves evaluating present practice, setting standards (guidelines/protocols), monitoring a chosen topic or standard, feedback of the findings, making changes in line with the outcomes and then resetting standards and further monitoring. Research is different in its purpose. It is a process of seeking knowledge through scientific inquiry. In other words the purpose of audit is to evaluate how closely our practice is to best practice, whereas research aims to establish what that best practice actually is (Firth-Cozens 1993).

Paxton (1995) identified several differences between audit and research. Research generally involves the principle of hypothesis testing and the random allocation of participants to different treatment groups. It occurs over a lengthy time span, includes large numbers of patients and frequently requires a rigorous use of statistical methods. Paxton indicated that audit normally requires none of these characteristics.

Edwards (1991) considered audit to be crude research which is quick and relatively easy to carry out. He stated that unless there was a marriage between audit and research "much audit will be sloppy and a waste of time". The differences that exist between audit and research clearly indicate that they are two different activities (Firth-Cozens 1996). Therefore, to directly compare audit with research and conclude that audit is a form of sloppy research is not justifiable. Audit is not research and stands as a process on its own.

Black (1992) described a number of examples of how audit and research interact with each other. He proposed that research should be the basis on which to develop standards to audit from: research may be used to measure the effectiveness of audit in attaining goals (i.e., "does audit improve services?" is a research question); and research may be audited by developing standards, for example, for methods of data collection in a research programme.

Roth & Fonagy (1996) in a study investigating psychotherapy approaches and clinical outcomes have developed a model linking research and audit for use in clinical practice (see Figure 1). Although the model describes a process to be used in psychotherapy, it has more general relevance for the interface between audit and research in the future. The model starts with clinicians developing innovative practice, leading onto the use of case series evaluation (or small pilot study) to further develop the idea. The next stage is the use of a randomised controlled trial (RCT) research project (based on the findings of the pilot). Once the RCT has demonstrated the efficacy of the treatment approach then standards and clinical guidelines can be developed for use in practice and for training. It also means that practice can be audited (using the guidelines) so clinicians can be shown to use treatment in a proper manner. The findings of NHS-commissioned research and development and critical appraisals of empirical research on treatment effectiveness are increasingly available, for example, through the NHS centres for reviews and dissemination and the Cochrane Collaboration (Marriott & Cape 1995).

The model demonstrates how research and audit can be complementary processes in the development of clinical guidelines to guide

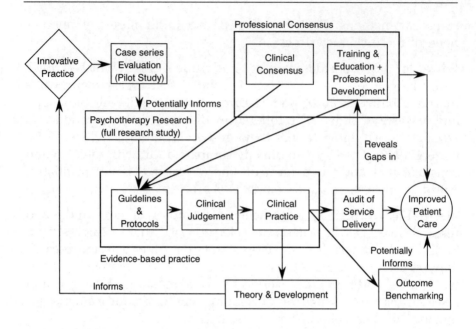

Figure 1 Roth & Fonagy's Model Linking Research and Audit. Reproduced by permission of Guilford Press

practice. Such guidelines in turn would provide the baseline criteria for audit purposes. Audit and research may have been, to date, distinct processes operating relatively independent of each other. However, when the processes are integrated there is the potential for a useful approach to measuring clinical effectiveness and outcome.

The use of audit within a framework of clinical effectiveness raises the particular question around measuring outcome. The development and use of measures of outcome must be subject to basic research issues of validity, reliability (Nunnally 1978) and generalisability (Cronbach et al 1972). The use of research methods to develop a means of measuring clinical outcome is important to ensure the legitimacy of audit findings.

It is beyond the remit of this book to discuss in detail aspects of research design and various approaches to measuring outcome validity, reliability and generalisability. However, for further reading useful texts include Barker et al (1994) and Cook & Campbell (1979).

CLINICAL GUIDELINES

Clinical practice guidelines (CPGs) may have a considerable impact on the practice of audit, and a programme of guideline development is being undertaken by the RCP/CRU and the CSAG at the Department of Health (Marriott & Lelliott 1994).

CPGs, often also referred to simply as "guidelines", are "systematically developed statements to assist practitioner and patient decisions about appropriate healthcare for specific clinical circumstances" (Field & Lohr 1990). They aim to enhance the guidance to clinicians on clinical practice which has traditionally been available through textbooks and articles or built into training curricula. There is some evidence that these sources may be inclined to inconsistency when compared to more objective, systematic reviews of available evidence (Antman et al 1992). CPGs aim to improve on traditional methods by using explicit documented processes to accurately reflect empirical findings, best clinical judgement and patient preferences.

CPGs also have a role in addressing variations in clinical practice and ensuring that care is appropriate. There is evidence of inconsistency in patterns of clinical care and concern that this reflects variations in the standards of care that patients receive (Hopkins 1993). For example, Marriott & Cape (1995) argue that type and length of treatment may have as much to do with the training and interest of the treating professional as with the characteristics of the patient. Considerations of equity as well as efficiency suggest that greater consistency of practice should be encouraged.

The specific clinical circumstances in which CPGs may be applied may be clinical conditions (e.g. assessment and treatment of obsessional problems), clinical issues (e.g. management of suspected child sexual abuse) or clinical procedures or interventions (e.g. implementation of behavioural programmes in residential settings).

CPGs refer specifically to the *process* of clinical care. They aim to define clinical processes that will lead to optimal health outcome. As CPGs contain statements about satisfactory performance they can be incorporated into clinical audit or QA studies as the standard against which actual performance can be measured.

To develop a guideline there has to be agreement on what is appropriate practice. The development of a guideline includes mechanisms, both to systematically evaluate the scientific evidence so that the guideline is valid, as well as to build consensus within the clinical community and with others who are affected by the guideline.

The most common originators of CPGs are either national professional bodies or groups of local clinicians. The evidence is that widespread CPG development is costly in time and resources (Brook 1989) and that locally developed protocols have greater acceptability while centrally developed ones have greater validity (Grimshaw & Russell 1993). It has therefore been suggested that local and national efforts should be co-ordinated. Authoritative, nationally developed CPGs could then be fleshed out and adapted to local circumstances (Clinical Resource and Audit Group 1993). The locally adapted protocol developed by local groups would then be given a term such as "local protocol" or "local guideline". Unlike the broad statement principle contained in the national guidelines, the local protocol would more closely describe the activity of health care professionals in day-to-day practice.

In the USA, government and professional organisations including the National Institute of Mental Health (the principal research funders in America) and the American Psychiatric Association are paying renewed interest to quality matters and the working of clinical protocols and practice guidelines. The American Association of Child and Adolescent Psychiatry (AACAP) has published practice guidelines on attention deficit hyperactivity disorder (ADHD), conduct disorders, anxiety disorders and (early onset) schizophrenia. The American Psychiatric Association (APA) has produced lengthy guidelines on eating disorders, major depression and bipolar disorder (Marriott & Lelliott 1994). The APA format for CPGs has broadly taken such headings as public significance of the illness, epidemiology, relevance, availability, attention to topic and so on and have been published as supplements to the *American Journal of Psychiatry* (Zarin et al 1993).

The UK may have been a relatively slow starter. However, in Scotland the Clinical Resource and Audit Group (CRAG), chaired by the Chief Medical Officer for Scotland, has produced a number of useful documents including a consensus statement on depressive illness written specifically for general practitioners (Clinical Research and Audit Group 1993), and a number of good practice statements for use by providers and purchasers, although they make it clear that these are not clinical guidelines. Areas covered so far include the management of delirium tremens and alcohol withdrawal (Clinical Research and Audit Group 1994), nursing observations of acutely ill patients (Clinical Research and Audit Group 1995a) and the management of schizophrenic patients (Clinical Research and Audit Group 1995b).

In the NHS in England the first major initiative was a trawl by the NHSE of extant CPGs, a number of which were commended as part of an executive letter on clinical effectiveness (NHSME 1993b). Further guidelines were included with the following year's circular on clinical effectiveness (NHSE 1994c). In the summer of 1994 the Clinical Guidelines Subgroup of the Clinical Outcomes Group was formed, with a remit of furthering the development of CPGs.

The advocates of CPGs argue that they will improve the effectiveness of health care and reduce inappropriate health care primarily through influencing clinicians' *behaviour*. To achieve the goal at least two conditions must be met. Firstly the CPG must be valid, that is, correctly define the clinical practices that will lead to optimal health outcome, and secondly the guideline must be acceptable to the clinician and to the patient:

Grimshaw & Russell (1994) reviewed dissemination and other strategies for getting medical practitioners to change, or to take note of CPGs. "Embedded" guidelines seemed to be effective as well as computer-generated reminders with non-compliant doctors. Guidelines can be disseminated in a variety of forms designed to suit the target audience, for instance as patient information sheets, or as clinical or educational tools.

CLINICAL INFORMATICS

Lack of information does constitute a major constraint to audit (Glover et al 1994, Knight 1995). "Clinical informatics" is defined as information systems that have the potential to support clinicians in implementing audit (Lelliott 1994b).

The need for local clinical information systems has stimulated large numbers of incompatible systems of varied quality and stages of development (Lelliott et al 1993). The Information Management Group (IMG) of the Department of Health has over the last few years sponsored a number of projects which aim to demonstrate the use of information management and technology in key areas of clinical care and service management. For example, the Community Information Systems for Providers (CISP) project concluded that information systems in the community must be

• *person based*, so that the health care record is held for each individual, which can then be referenced to the individual's NHS number;
• *integrated*, so that duplicated data entry is minimised and information is available in other designated NHS systems;
• *operational*, and aimed at supporting clinical work so that additional efforts required to capture information specifically for management purposes is minimised; and
• *secure*, so that information is only made available on the "need to know" basis to authorised staff.

Wing (1992) states that progress towards clinical and administrative targets specified as operational measures can only be achieved accurately if there is a common mental health information system (MHIS) serving the following types of function:

1. Individual patient care; clinical assessment (symptoms, behaviour, social disablement); social assessment (social circumstances, family, occupation, house, income); life history; treatment care and welfare plans, care environment; Mental Health Act; discharge letters after care, liaison and clinical outcomes.
2. Multi-agency contacts, resource management, planning and reports to contractors.
3. Public health and social service (purchaser) functions such as geographical needs assessment, planning and targeting, contracts, monitoring of quality control of services, epidemiology.
4. Central returns.

The measurement of clinical and administrative targets requires complementary methods. Clinical targets are those relating to the delivery of specified care to individual users assessed as being in need, the anticipated reduction in symptoms, behavioural signs and social disablement and improvement in quality of life. Administrative targets on the other hand are defined in terms of agents and agencies: number of places or staff, length of stay, waiting times, patients or clients seen, MHIS put in place, area regional or national targets achieved.

Of the two the achievement of administrative targets is relatively easier to assess given a good-quality MHIS, since they are usually couched in terms of numbers and categories that are fairly easy to ascertain. Clinical targets are more problematic as they usually involve the measurement complexities discussed above.

The aim of the minimum data set (Lelliott 1995) will be to change the focus of information on administration to patient care. Information will be recorded about patient care when clinical planning and reviews *occur*. A minimum data set is a set of items for information which all providers of any type of service in the NHS would need to collect to do their work. By introducing a standardised structure and set of definitions, the Department of Health can then ensure that this information is aggregated and comparisons made reliably on a national basis.

Read codes are a set of coded clinical terms that arc nationally agreed and developed by and for clinicians. The terms are coded for use in person-based computerised systems and provide clinical audit research information and decision support. Such a system is essential if comprehensive data about clinical encounters is to be captured in computers. Without the capture of such data the electronic patient record is impossible and will remain a severely restricted source of data for audit, outcomes, care protocols, management of resources and contracting. Recent work has successfully expanded the Read codes to become an agreed thesaurus of clinical terms, synonyms and abbreviations initially for the medical profession. The project involved establishing 43 speciality working groups representing every medical specialty, including mental health. A total of 2000 clinicians and over 55 working groups have been involved in these projects, co-ordinated by the NHS Centre for Coding and Classification.

The thesaurus itself is a large structured database containing health care record terms (agreed by all the health care professions). The terms are in clinical use, and use natural language as opposed to "classification speak". The ultimate aim of the thesaurus is to provide a lexicon of terms for clinicians, nurses and other professions allied to medicine to insert into patient-centred records. The codes themselves are merely electronic tags for "core concepts", for which preferred terms and synonyms are provided. The database is structured in a hierarchical fashion. A "child" term is a "subtype" of the "parent" term to which it is linked. These parent–child links form the skeletal structure of the database. When added to the brief scales for measuring outcome (HoNOS) the promise is of a comprehensive information system that will routinely record all the principal aspects of care and ensuing outcomes (Lelliott 1995).

Some professionals may feel that IT is no more than another irritating interference in the core business of direct patient care. Taking a lead role over an inevitable change can only increase the later "ownership", and control of the purposes to which data analysis is put. Clinicians need to take an active interest in such developments as they are central to the matter of information and measurement in mental health (McClelland 1995).

USER INVOLVEMENT IN AUDIT

The involvement of service users in audit has developed rather slowly. Patients have been involved in the measurement of patient satisfaction with general care provided or perceived change in health status outcomes (Ross-Davies 1994). Patient views on what is a good outcome might be different from those who care for them (Firth-Cozens 1993). Some form of dialogue needs to be established between service users and providers to enable services to become more responsive to user needs (Barker & Peck 1987).

The Patients' Association have expressed a need for open access to audit information. Professionals may feel that the lack of understanding of technical matters amongst lay people, the emphasis placed on confidentiality amongst their peers and the shifting of focus to "patient" issues justify a policy of restricted access to audit data.

Rigge (1994) suggested that statements like "the quality of medical work can only be reviewed by a doctor's peer" (*Working Paper 6,* 1989) made it initially difficult for patients to have a more central role in audit or other types of quality reviews of clinical practice. She raised the question of how patients can be involved in clinical audit without being "marginalised", and suggested that the patient could have a more central place if the necessary training and support were available. Users could have a major role in a range of qualitative methods, including:

Interviewing
- In-depth interviews with patient and carers in their own homes
- Interviews with staff at every level (including medical records clerks and secretaries)

"Focus groups" with
- members of voluntary organisations
- ethnic or cultural minority groups
- other potential service user groups (who have not gained access to services, for whatever reason)

The Newcastle project involved mental health service clients in developing a new system of clinical audit (The *Newcastle Audit System for Mental Health;* Balogh & Bond 1995). The clients were involved in specifying and validating audit topics, as members of the audit team and as the subjects of data collection. The Newcastle system is based on the principle that care providers must be involved in clinical audit, along with clients and other agencies. The system was developed in response to existing mental health systems, involving clients in audit only to provide information (Balogh et al 1993). The aim was not only to develop client participatory methods but also more enpowering methods of asking clients their views on the care they received.

The RCP/CRU has involved users in the development of its first CPG (on the management of violence). They are to be included in developmental and steering groups for future CPG work. Users' views were sought on which areas needed CPGs. Their intention was to ensure user understanding of CPGs.

Service users are those best placed to judge on access, process and outcome of a service. They have a unique perspective of the care process essential to any complete service evaluation (Stallard &

Chadwick 1991, McAuliffe & MacLachlan 1992). There are a number of ways in which service user involvement in clinical audit and quality steering groups may be helpful, including involvement in identifying issues (on clinical audit groups), as surveyors of other users, to identify user outcomes/perceptions of effectiveness and to identify user information needs. Their involvement would benefit service providers by informing others, including users, about the services, increasing accountability of the service, providing feedback to others, and promoting partnerships. The development of future audit/QA programmes would without question need to involve service users in a central capacity.

THE INVOLVEMENT OF PURCHASERS

Clinical audit was originally professionally led and was not subject to contracting between purchaser and providers. To date purchasers have not been involved in clinical audit to any great degree (Packwood & Kober 1995, BMA 1996). However, purchasers have a responsibility to ensure that audit continues to develop (NHSE 1995) and to begin to incorporate their interests in the process (Thomson et al 1993). The most significant change in recent years has been the change in funding source (Cape 1995). From 1994–5 the previous ring fencing of audit funding ceased, and units and trusts received their audit funding from purchasers rather than directly from Region. About 2% of an average trust budget is spent on audit and such a proportion of spending is likely to continue (Thomson et al 1996). Clinical audit will ultimately be funded through contracts for clinical services (National Audit Office 1995) and in competition with other demands for resources. Information on how purchasers are beginning to influence clinical audit is only now beginning to emerge (Rumsey et al 1993). Purchasers may expect to agree the future audit programmes with providers before funding is released.

Clinical audit has changed since 1989 from its original and primary focus around the education of professionals. Clinical audit is no longer a process in itself but is linked to other parallel developments. For example, trusts tend to link audit to other aspects of quality management and purchasers increasingly view it as a means for demonstrating outcomes and clinical effectiveness. Littlejohn

(1996) summarises the types of audit that currently exist as being either "isolationist" (professionally led and dominated) or "integrated" (that is, managers and professionals deciding areas to be studied and pursuing these in line with organisational requirements). However, a third way is also possible, namely, an "intermediate" model (a mixture of the two). Such a solution has been further encouraged by recent guidance (NHSME 1994) which suggests that 40% of audit projects should be chosen by commissioners, 40% from within audit departments and the remaining 20% split between national audit and audit across the primary/secondary care interface (BMA 1996).

It has been argued that audit can only achieve its potential when purchasers' interests are incorporated into the audit process (Harmen & Martin 1992, Thomson & Barton 1994). This is reasonable as purchasers may need to be involved to foster change. It has been a central argument of this book that neither service monitoring nor audit can itself bring change. Data must be placed in the hands of someone who can do something with it. Developing a collaboration with providers may result in more effective clinical audit programmes and quality initiatives being written into clinical service contracts.

Purchasers and providers have important differences in their views on the level and appropriateness of involvement of health care purchasers in clinical audit (Thomson et al 1996). Providers tend to think that for audit to achieve its purpose more protected time for clinicians, information technology, support staff and additional resources are required. Purchasers, on the other hand, have a slightly different agenda and would wish audit to become a means of showing outcome and efficiency, reflecting their purchasing priorities.

There is concern that clinical ownership may be diminished by the increasing involvement of purchasers, and it is not clear to what extent the data and conclusions of clinical audit studies should be shared and the degree to which participants should remain anonymous. Clinicians and providers strongly assert that audit should be confidential and the identity of individual clinicians protected (Thomson et al 1996).

CPGs are a recent development, strongly endorsed by the Department of Health as a strand in its strategy to promote clinical effectiveness through both purchasers and clinical service providers (NHSME 1993b and NHSSE 1994). CPGs also have a role to play in purchasing and quality monitoring. They offer the possibility of embedding clinical issues much more securely at the centre of the commissioning process than has so far been possible. Purchaser involvement may include prioritising areas for the introduction of local guidelines, incorporating guidelines into service specifications, supporting providers in implementing guidelines, and monitoring the achievement of the standards of care specified in the guidelines.

Review and dissemination of best practice may lead to "evidence-based purchasing". Such evidence could be seen as a way of helping purchasers overcome their lack of knowledge about specific treatments and approaches. Provider-generated information (however detailed) may always be insufficient to satisfy health authorities that appropriate care has been offered.

There is the further issue of how health authorities can seek to optimise outcomes – a particular difficulty in mental health, as evidence of the effectiveness of interventions in the community is scant and accountability for the "severely mentally ill" is not clear. It is difficult, therefore, for purchasers to focus on any one intervention or type of person, and variations in outcome may simply reflect different inputs, for example the qualifications and experience of key workers and case managers.

However, from the point of view of purchasers, evidence-based medicine has its constraints. Health authorities are still left with the big problem of interpretation, for which they are ultimately dependent on professionals (Klein 1995), and statistical interpretation of audit work is complicated by factors such as case mix, with some clinicians and services carrying more difficult and complex cases and therefore only appearing to have poorer outcomes.

In short, purchasers (now often the combined Health Authority/ Family Health Services Authority) are likely to require more multidisciplinary audit and a change to a more measurement-orientated culture. The need for a cultural change and for a multidisciplinary approach seems generally agreed (BMA 1996). They will expect the greater involvement of managers whilst maintaining the professional ownership of audit. Uniprofessional audit will have a much smaller but still significant role. Joint audit between primary and secondary care sectors and with social services is likely to be encouraged. Contracting will become more audit and information based, with monitoring taking place not just on numbers but on treatments given, services delivered and outcomes achieved.

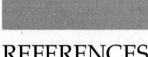

REFERENCES

Aidroos, N. (1991). Use of and effectiveness of psychiatric nursing care plans. *Journal of Advanced Nursing*, **16**, 177–181.

Anderson, J. (1991). User satisfaction, user participation and evaluation of mental health services: Experiences in the USA and Britain. In *National Perspectives on Quality Assurance in Mental Health Care*. Geneva: World Health Organization.

Antman, E., Lau, J. & Kupelnick, B. et al (1992). A comparison of results of meta-analyses of randomised control trials and recommendations of clinical experts: Treatments for myocardial infarction. *Journal of the American Medical Association*. **268**, 240–248.

Ashbaugh, J. (1990) The role of performance contracts in quality assurance. In Bradley, V. and Bersani, H. (eds), *Quality Assurance for Individuals with Developmental Disabilities*. Baltimore, MD: Brookes.

Atkinson, C. & Hayden, J. (1992). Strategies for success. *British Medical Journal*, **304**, 1488–1490.

Attkisson, C.C. & Zwick, R. (1982). The client satisfaction questionnaire: Psychometric properties and correlations with service utilization and psychotherapy outcome. *Evaluation and Programme Planning*, **5**, 233–237.

Audini, B. & Lelliott, P. (1966). *Problems with the CPA: An Interview Survey of 62 Provider Services*. Royal College of Psychiatrists Research Unit.

Bachrach, L. (1996). Managed care: Whose business is patient care? *Psychiatric Services*, **47**(6), 567–576.

Baker, A. (1976). The Hospital Advisory Service. In McLachlan, G. (ed.), *A Question of Quality*. London: Oxford University Press, 203–216.

Baker, R. & Whitfield, M. (1992). Measuring patient satisfaction: A test of construct validity. *Quality in Health Care*, **1**, 104–109.

Balogh, R. & Bond, S. (1995). Telling it like it is. *Health Service Journal*, March, 26–27.

Balogh, R., Simpson, A., Quinn, H. & Bond, S. (1993). *An Analysis of Instruments and Tools Used in Psychiatric Audit*. Report No. 62. Centre for Health Services Research, Newcastle University.

Balogh, R., Simpson, A. & Bond, S. (1996). Involving clients in clinical audit of mental health services. *International Journal for Quality in Health Care*, **7**(4), 343–353.

Bamford, C. & Jacoby, A. (1992). Development of patient satisfaction questionnaires: 1. Methodological issues. *Quality in Health Care*, **1**, 153–157.

Barker, C., Pistrang, N. & Elliot, R. (1994). *Research Methods in Clinical and Counselling Psychology*. Chichester: Wiley.

Barker, I. & Peck, E. (1987). *Power in Strange Places: User Empowerment in Mental Health Services*. London: GPMH.

Barkham, M. & Shapiro, D.A. (1989). Towards resolving the problem of waiting lists: Psychotherapy in two-plus-one sessions. *Clinical Psychology Forum*, **23**, 15–18.

Barrie, J. & Marsh, D. (1992). Quality of data in the Manchester Orthopaedic Database. *British Medical Journal*, **304**, 159–162.

Bebbington, P.E., Feeney, S.T., Flannigan, C.B., Glover, G.R., Lewis, S.W. & Wing, J.K. (1994). Inner London Collaborative Audit of admissions. II. Ethnicity and the use of the Mental Health Act. *British Journal of Psychiatry*, **165**, 734–749.

Beck, A.T. (1987). *Beck Depression Inventory: Manual*. San Antonio, TX: Psychological Corporation.

Beck, A.T. & Steer, R.A. (1987). *Manual of the Revised Beck Depression Inventory:* San Antonio, TX: Psychological Corporation.

Beck, A.T., Ward, C.H., Mendelson, M., Mock, J. & Erbaugh, J. (1961). An inventory for measuring depression. *Archives of General Psychiatry*, **4**, 561–571.

Beck, A.T., Epstein, N., Brown, G. & Steer, R.A. (1988). An inventory for measuring clinical anxiety: Psychometric properties. *Journal of Consulting and Clinical Psychology*, **56**, 893–897.

Berwick, D. (1992). Continuous quality improvement in medicine: From theory to practice. *Quality in Health Care* **1** (suppl.).

Black, N. (1992). The relationship between evaluative research and audit. *Journal of Public Mental Health Medicine*, **14**, 361–366.

Blom-Cooper, L., Hally, H. & Murphy, E. (1995). The falling shadow: One patient's mental health care 1978–1993. London: HMSO.

Brazier, J.E., Harper, R., Jones, N.B.M., O'Cathian, A., Thomas, K.J., Usherwood, T. & Westlake, L. (1992). Validating the SF-36 health survey questionnaire: A new outcome measure for primary care. *British Medical Journal*, **305**, 160–164.

Brink, T., Yesavage, J.A., Lum, O., Heersema, P.H., Adey, M. & Rose, T.S. (1982). Screening tests for geriatric depression. *Clinical Gerontologist*, **1**, 37–43.

British Medical Association (1996). *Guidance Notes for the Commissioning of Clinical Audit*. London: BMA.

Brook, R.H. (1989) Practice guidelines and practicing medicine: Are they compatible? *Journal of the American Medical Association*, **262**, 3027–3031.

Brooks, T. (1992). Success through organisational audit. *Health Services Management*, **88**(8), 13–15.

Brooks, T. (1994). The Kings Fund Organisational Audit. *Kings Fund News*, **17**(3), 1–3.

Brown, J. & Simpson, L. (1992). *Critical Paths*. Presented at "Partnership in Audit" Conference, York (November).

Bucknall, A. (1994). Evaluation of a client satisfaction questionnaire. *Clinical Psychology Forum*, **63**, 22–26.

Bullmore, E., Joyce, H., Marks, I. & Kie, J. (1992). A computerised quality assurance system (QAS) on general psychiatric ward: Towards efficient clinical audit. *Journal of Mental Health*, **1**, 257–263.

Burke, W.W. (1982). *Organization Development: Principles and Practice*. Boston, MA: Little, Brown.

Burn et al, (1992). In the *International Journal of Geriatric Psychiatry*.

Buttery, Y., Walshe, K., Coles, J. & Bennett, J. (1993). *The Development of Audit: Findings of a National Survey of Healthcare Provider Units in England*. London: CASPE.

Buttery, Y., Walshe, K., Coulds, J. & Bennett, J. (1994). *Evaluating Medical Audit. The Development of Audit: Findings of a National Survey of Healthcare Provider Units in England*. London: CASPE.

Buttery, Y., Walshe, K., Ramsey, M., Amoss, M., Bennett, J. & Coles, J. (1995).

Provider audit in England: A review of twenty-nine programmes. London: CASPE.

Caldicott, F. (1994). Letter to the Secretary of State for Health. *Psychiatric Bulletin*, **18**, 385–386.

Campling, E., Devlin, H., Hoile, R. & Lunn, J. (eds) (1993). *The Report of the National Enquiry into Perioperative Deaths 1991/92*. London: NCEPOD.

Cape, J. (1995). Clinical audit in the NHS. *Clinical Psychology Forum*, **86**, 12–16.

Chambers, R., Bowyer, S. & Campbell, I. (1995). Audit activity and quality of completed audit projects in primary care in Staffordshire. *Quality in Health Care*, **4**, 178–183.

Chambers, R., Bowyer, S. & Campbell, I. (1996). Investigation into the attitudes of general practitioners in Staffordshire to Medical Audit. *Quality in Health Care*, **5**, 13–19.

Christie, G. & Francis, S. (1987). An introductory out-patient group for patients on the Cassel Hospital in-patient waiting list. *Psychoanalytic Psychotherapy*, **2**(3), 227–245.

Clarke, D.M. (1989). Anxiety states: panic and generalized anxiety. In Hawton, K., Salkovskis, P.M., Kirk, J. & Clarke, D.M. (eds) *Cognitive Behaviour Therapy for Psychiatric Problems: A Practical Guide*. Oxford: Oxford University Press.

Clifford, P. (1996). *Structuring the Clinical Record: The FACE Assessment and Outcome System: Main Report*. London: BPS.

Clifford, P., Leiper, R., Lavender, A. & Pilling, S. (1989). *Assuring Quality in Mental Health Services: The QUARTZ System*. London: Free Association.

Clinical Resource and Audit Group (1993). *Depressive Illness: A Critical Review of Current Practice and the Way Ahead*. Scottish Office, NHS Scotland (June).

Clinical Resource and Audit Group (1994). *The Management of Alcohol Withdrawal and Delerium Tremens: A good practice statement*. Scottish Office, NHS Scotland (June).

Clinical Resource and Audit Group (1995a). *Nursing Observation of Acutely Ill Psychiatric Patients in Hospital*. Scottish Office, NHS Scotland, (May).

Clinical Resource and Audit Group (1995b). *Services for People Affected by Schizophrenia: A Good Practice Statement*. Scottish Office, NHS Scotland (March).

Coch, L. & French, J.P.R., Jr (1948). Overcoming resistance to change. *Human Relations*, **11**, 512–532.

College Research Unit (1996). *Annual Report 1995: Marking the First Five Years*. London: Royal College of Psychiatrists.

Conning, A. & Rowland, L. (1992). Staff attitudes and the provision of individualised care: What determines what people do for people with long term psychiatric disabilities? *Journal of Mental Health*, **1**, 71–80.

Cook, T.D. & Campbell, D.T. (1979). *Quasi-experimentation: Design and Analysis issues for Field Settings*. Boston, MA: Houghton Mifflin.

Cowan, C. (1991). Multidisciplinary involvement in hospital discharge: A regional survey of current practice in general adult psychiatry. *Psychiatric Bulletin*, **15**, 415–416.

Crombie, I., Davis, H., Abraham, S. & Florey, C. (1993). *The Audit Handbook: Improving Healthcare Through Clinical Audit*. Chichester: Wiley.

Cronbach, L.J., Gleser, G.C., Nanda, H. & Rajaratnam, N. (1972). *The Dependability of Behavioural Measurements: Theory of Generalizability of Scores and Profiles*. New York: Wiley.

CSAG (1995). *Clinical Standards Advisory Group: Schizophrenia* (Vol. 1). London: HMSO.

Cunnane, J. (1994). Drug management of disturbed behaviour by psychiatrists. *Psychiatric Bulletin*, **18**, 138–139.

Dale, B.G. & Plunkett, J.J. (1991). *Quality Costing*. London: Chapman & Hall.

Dale, B.G., Lascelles, D.M. & Plunkett, J.J. (1990). *The process of Total Quality Management*. In Dale, B.G. & Plunkett, J.J. (eds), *Managing Quality*, London: Philip Allan.

Davies, N., Ringham, R., Prior, C. & Simms, A. (1995). *Reports of the enquiry into the circumstances leading to the death of Jonathan Newby (a volunteer worker) on the 9 October 1993 in Oxford*. London: HMSO.

Dawson, J., Fitzpatrick, R., Murray, D. & Carr, A. (1996). A comparison of measures to assess outcomes in total hip replacement surgery. *Quality in Health Care*, **5**, 81–88.

De Dombal, F. (1994). What is wrong with medical audit? *Medical Audit News* **4**(8), 117–120.

Delany, N. (1992). Good Practice in ECT. *Psychiatric Bulletin*, **16**, 272–273.

Denman, F. (1994). Quality in a psychotherapy service: A review of audio tapes of sessions. *Psychiatric Bulletin*, **18**, 80–82.

Department of Health (1989a). *Medical Audit. Working Paper 6: Working for Patients*. London: HMSO.

Department of Health (1989b). *Discharge Planning* (HC/89;5). London: HMSO.

Department of Health (1989c). *Caring for People* (CM 849). London: HMSO.

Department of Health (1990a). *Care Programme Approach* (HC/90/23). London: HMSO.

Department of Health (1990b). *Caring for People: The Care Programme Approach for People with a Mental Illness Referred to the Specialist Psychiatric Services* (HC/90/23/LASS(90)11.1990. London: HMSO.

Department of Health (1992). *The Health of the Nation: A Strategy of Health in England*. London: HMSO.

Department of Health (1993a). *Clinical Audit Initiative: Funding for 1994/5 and beyond*. London: HMSO.

Department of Health (1993b). *Clinical Audit: Meeting and Improving Standards in Healthcare*. London: HMSO.

Department of Health (1994a). *The Health of the Nation. Key Area Handbook: Mental Illness* (2nd edn). London: HMSO.

Department of Health (1994b). *Introduction of Supervision Registers for Mentally Ill People* (HSG(94)5). London: HMSO.

Department of Health (1995). *Building Bridges: A Guide to Arrangements for Inter-Agency Working for the Care and Protection of Severely Mentally Ill People*. Department of Health, Wetherby, Yorkshire.

Department of Health (1996). *An Audit Pack for Monitoring the Care Programme Approach*. London: HMSO.

Derogatis, L.R., Lipman, R.S. & Covi, M.D. (1973). SCL-90: An outpatient rating scale: Preliminary report. *Psychopharmacology Bulletin*, **9**, 13–20.

Devlin, B. (1996). *The Royal Colleges*. Paper given at the Second National Conference on Audit and Mental Health Services, Sheffield, February.

Diamond, H., Tislow, R., Snyder, T & Ricknells, K. (1975). Peer review of prescribing patterns in CMHC. *American Journal of Psychiatry*, **133**, 697–699.

Dickens, P. (1994). *Quality and Excellence in Human Services*. Chichester: Wiley.

Division of Clinical Psychology (1993). Report of the DCP survey of waiting lists in NHS Clinical Psychology Services: 1992. *Clinical Psychology Forum*, **53**, 39–42.

Dixon, N. (1989). *A Guide to Medical Audit*. Hereford: National Association of Quality Assurance in Health Care.

Dombal, F.T. de (1994). What is wrong with Medical Audit. *Medical Audit News*, **4**(8), 117–120.

Donabedian, A. (1980). The definition of quality: A conceptual exploration. in Donabedian, A. (ed.), *Explorations in Quality Assessment and Monitoring*. Ann Arbor, MI: Health Administration Press.

Donabedian, A. (1982). *Explorations in Quality Assessment and Monitoring, Vol. 2: The Criteria and Standards of Quality*. Ann Arbor, MI: Health Administration Press.

Donabedian, A. (1988). The quality of care: how can it be assessed? *Journal of the American Medical Association*, **260**, 1743–1748.

Dotchin, J.A. & Oakland, J.S. (1992). Theories and concepts in Total Quality Management. *Total Quality Management*, **3**(2), 133–145.

Double, D. (1991). What has happened to patients from long stay psychiatric wards? *Psychiatric Bulletin*, **15**, 735–736.

Dunnett, C.W. (1955). A multiple comparison procedure for comparing several treatments with a control. *Journal of the American Statistical Association*, **50**, 1096–1121.

Dutta, A., Parker, R.R. & Fleet, T.W. (1991). Audit in two acute psychiatric units. *Psychiatric Bulletin*, **15**, 351–352.

Eagly, A.H., Wood, W. & Chaiken, S. (1978). Causal inferences about communicators and their effect on opinion change. *Journal of Personality and Social Psychology*, **36**, 424–435.

Edwards, G. (1991). Audit in practice: A decade of psychiatric audit in Southampton. *Psychiatric Bulletin*, **15**, 732–734.

Elkin, I. (1994). The NIMH treatment of depression collaborative research programme: Where we began and where we are. In Bergin, A.E. & Garfield, S.L. (eds), *Handbook of Psychotherapy and Behaviour Change* (4th edn). New York: Wiley. 114–139.

Elkin, I., Shea, T., Watkins, J.T., Imber, S.D., Sotsky, S.M., Collins, J.F., Glass, D.R., Pilkonis, P.A., Leber, W.R., Docherty, J.P., Fiester, S.J. & Parloff, M.B. (1989). National Institute of Mental Health treatment of depression collaborative programme: General effectiveness of treatments. *Archives of General Psychiatry*, **46**, 971–982.

Ellis, R. (1988). *Professional Competence and Quality Assurance in the Caring Professions*. London: Chapman & Hall.

Endicott, J., Spitzer, R.L., Fleiss, J.L. & Cohen, J. (1976). The Global Assessment Scale: A procedure for measuring overall severity of psychiatric disturbance. *Archives of General Psychiatry*, **33**, 766–771.

Evans, M.D., Hollon, S.D., DeRubeis, R.J., Piasecki, J.M., Grove, W.M., Garvey, M.J. & Turson, V.B. (1992). Differential relapse following cognitive therapy and pharmacotherapy for depression. *Archives of General Psychiatry*, **49**, 802–808.

Feenan (1994) in the *International Journal of Geriatric Psychiatry* (Abstract Rev.).

Field, M.J. & Lohr, K.N. (1990). *Clinical Practice Guidelines: Directions for a New Programme*. Washington, DC: National Academy Press.

Finnegan, E. (1992). *Collaborative Care Planning: A Revolutionary New Model for Effective Patient Management*: West Midlands.

Firth-Cozens, J. (1992). Building effective teams for audit. *Quality in Health Care*, **1**, 161–164.

Firth-Cozens, J. (1993). *Audit in Mental Health Services*. Hove: Erlbaum.

Firth-Cozens, J. (1996). Looking at effectiveness: Ideas from the couch. *Quality in Health Care*, **5**, 55–59.

Firth-Cozens, J. & Ennis, W. (1995). Marriage guidance: The relationship between research and audit. *Health Service Journal*, **10** (August), 24–25.

Fitzpatrick, R. (1991). Surveys of patient satisfaction: I. Important general considerations. *British Medical Journal*, **302**, 887–889.

Fitzpatrick, R., Ziebland, S., Jenkinson, C., Mowat, A. & Mowat, A. (1992). Importance of sensitivity to change as a criteria for selecting health status measurement. *Quality in Health Care*, **1**, 89–93.

Flannigan, C.B., Glover, G.R., Feeney, S.T., Wing, J.K., Bebbington, P.E. & Lewis, S.W. (1994a). Inner London Collaborative Audit of admissions. I. Introduction, methods and preliminary findings. *British Journal of Psychiatry*, **165**, 734–743.

Flannigan, C.B., Glover, G.R., Wing, J.K., Lewis, S.W., Bebbington, P.E. & Feeney, S.T. (1994b). Inner London Collaborative audit of admissions. III. Reasons for acute admission to psychiatric wards. *British Journal of Psychiatry*, **165**, 750–759.

Fonagy, P. & Higgitt, A. (1989). Evaluating the performance of departments of psychotherapy. *Psychoanalytic Psychotherapy*, **4**, 121–153.

Foster, J., Willmot, M. & Coles, J. (1996). *Nursing and Therapy Audit: An Evaluation of Twenty Four Projects and Initiatives.* London: CASPE.

Fowkes, F.G.R. (1982). Medical Audit Cycle. *Medical Education*, **16**, 228–238.

Frost, D. (1995). *Outcome Measures in Mental Health.* University College London Medical School Department of Psychiatry, Camden and Islington Mental Health Service Trust.

Frost, D. & Monteith, K. (1996). About FACE. *Health Service Journal*, February, 30–32.

Garnick, D. & Comstock, C. (1996). Measuring quality of care: Fundamental information from administrative datasets. *International Journal for Quality in Health Care*, **6**, 163–177.

Garratt, A.M., Ruta, D.A., Abdalla, M.I., Buckingham, J.K. & Russell, I.T. (1993). The SF-36 health survey questionnaire: An outcome measure suitable for routine use within the NHS? *British Medical Journal*, **306**, 1140–1143.

Gath, A. (1991). Audit. *Psychiatric Bulletin*, **15**, 23–35.

Gilleard, C. (1995). Implementation of the care programme approach in the community. *Psychiatric Bulletin*, **19**, 750–752.

Gilles, A. (1996). Improving patient care in the UK: Clinical Audit in the Oxford region. *International Journal for Quality in Health Care*, **8**(2), 141–152.

Glover, G.R. (1989). The pattern of psychiatric admissions of Caribbean born immigrants in London. *Social Psychiatry and Psychiatric Epidemiology*, **24**, 49–56.

Glover, G.R. (1990a). Medical Audit in Mental Health Care. *Psychiatric Bulletin*, **14**, 326–327.

Glover, G.R. (1990b). The audit of mental health services. *Quality Assurance in Health Care*, **2**, 181–188.

Glover, G.R. (1991). The use of in-patient psychiatric care by immigrants in a London Borough. *International Journal of Social Psychiatry*, **37**, 121–134.

Glover, G. (1994) *National Perspectives and Developments in Audit in Mental Health.* Paper given at The Cutting Edge of Practice: National Conference on Audit in Mental Health Services, Cutler's Hall, Sheffield, November.

Glover, G.R. (1995). Information systems for mental health care: Uses, shapes and rhythms. *Advances in Psychiatric Treatment*, **1**, 237–242.

Glover, G.R., Robin, E., Emami, J. & Arabsheibani, G. (1994a). *The Distribution of Need for Mental Health Services: A Study of the Socio Demographic Predictors of Prevalence of Psychiatric Hospital Admission in the London Region.* London: Royal College of Psychiatrists Research Unit.

Glover, G.R., Flannigan, C.B., Feeney, S.T., Wing, J.K., Bebbington, P.E. & Lewis, S.W. (1994b). Admission of British Caribbeans to psychiatric hospitals: Is it a cohort effect? *Social Psychiatry and Psychiatry Epidemiology*, **29**, 282–284.

Godber, G. (1975). *The Health Service: Past, Present and Future*. London: Athlone Press.

Goldberg, D.P. (1978). *Manual of the General Health Questionnaire*. Windsor: NFER.

Gournay, K. (1994). Redirecting the emphasis to serious mental illness. *Nursing Times*, **90**(25), 40–41.

Green, S. (1992). *Measuring Outcomes in the Mental Health Services*. HSMC, University of Birmingham.

Griffiths, R. (1983). *NHS Management Inquiry*. London: DHSS.

Grimshaw, J. & Russell, I. (1993). Achieving health gain through clinical guidelines. I. Developing scientifically valid guidelines. *Quality in Health Care*, **2**, 243–248.

Grimshaw, J. & Russell, I. (1994). Achieving health gain through clinical guidelines. II. Ensuring that guidelines change medical practice. *Quality in Health Care*, **3**, 45–52.

Gupta, N. (1995). Keyworkers and the care programme approach: The role and responsibilities of community workers. *Psychiatric Care*, **1**(6), 239–242.

Hardy, G.E., West, M.A. & Hill, F. (1996). Components and predictors of patient satisfaction. *British Journal of Health Psychology*, **1**, 65–85.

Harmen, D. & Martin, G. (1992). Managers and medical audit. *Health Services Management*, **88**(2), 27–29.

Harrison, G., Owens, D., Holton, A., Neilson, D. & Boot, D. (1988). A prospective study of severe mental disorder in Afro-Caribbean patients. *Psychological Medicine*. **18**, 643–657.

Hatton, P. & Renvoize, E. (1992). A framework for psychiatric audit. *Medical Audit News*, **2**(2), 40–41.

Hayes, V., Morris, J., Wolfe, C. & Morgan, M. (1995). The SF-36 health survey questionnaire: Is it suitable for use with older adults? *Age and Ageing*, **24**, 120–125.

Hearnshaw, H., Baker, R. & Robertson, N. (1994). Multidisciplinary audit in primary healthcare teams: Facilitation by audit support staff. *Quality in Health Care*, **3**, 164–168.

Hobbs, K.E.F. (1994). Clinical Audit: A £210 million bandwagon. *Medical Audit News*, **4**, 121–123.

Hollander, D. & Slater, M. (1994). "Sorry no beds": A problem for acute psychiatric admissions. *Psychiatric Bulletin*, **18**, 532–534.

Hollon, S.D., DeRubeis, R.J., Evans, M.D., Wiemer, M.J., Gargey, M.J., Grove, W.M. & Turson, V.B. (1992). Cognitive therapy and pharmacotherapy for depression: Singly or in combination. *Archives of General Psychiatry*, **49**, 774–781.

Hopkins, A. (1993). Report of a working group: What do we mean by appropriate health care? *Quality in Health Care*, **2**, 117–123.

Hornby, S. (1993). *Collaborative Care: Interprofessional, Interagency and Interpersonal*. Oxford: Blackwell Scientific Publications.

Houghton, A., Bowling, A., Clarke, K.D., Hopkins, A.P. & Jones, I. (1996). Does a dedicated discharge co-ordinator improve the quality of hospital discharge. *Quality in Health Care*, **5**, 89–96.

Hunt, S.M., McKenna, S.P., McEwen, J., Williams, J. & Papp, E. (1981). The Nottingham Health Profile: Subjective health status and medical consultations. *Social Science and Medicine*, **15**, 221–229.

Hurst, J. (1992). *The Reform of Health Care: A Comparative Analysis of Seven OECD Countries*. Paris: OECD.

Hyer, L. & Blount, J. (1984). Concurrent and discriminant validities of the GDS with older psychiatric patients. *Psychological Reports*, **54**, 611–616.

Ineichen, B., Harrison, G. & Morgan, H.G. (1984). Psychiatric hospital admissions in

Bristol. I. Geographical and ethnic factors. *British Journal of Psychiatry*, **145**, 600–604.

Jenkins, R. (1990). Towards a system of outcome indicators for mental health care. *British Journal of Psychiatry*, **157**, 500–514.

Jenkins, R. (1994). The Health of the Nation: Recent Government policy and legislation. *Psychiatric Bulletin*, **18**, 324–327.

Jenkins, R. (1996). *What next with clinical audit?* Paper given at Clinical Audit in Psychiatry Conference, Royal College of Psychiatrists Research Unit, London.

Jenkinson, C. (1994). Quality of life measurement: Does it have a place in routine clinical assessment? *Journal of Psychosexual Research*, **38**, 377–381.

Jenkinson, C., Coulter, A. & Wright, L. (1993). Short Form-36 (SF-36) health survey questionnaire: Normative data for adults of working age. *British Medical Journal*, **306**, 1437–1440.

Johnson, A. (1992). Audit and ethics. *Medical Audit News*, **2**(8), 119–120.

Johnson, J. & DiBona, J. (1990). A concurrent quality assurance review of psychotrophic prescribing in elderly patients: Process and outcome measures. *Journal of Geriatric Drug Therapy*, **4**, 43–80.

JCAH (1989). Factors that determine quality of patient care. *Quality Review Bulletin*, **15**(11), 331.

Jones, E. (1991). Audit in psychiatry: "Failed discharges". *Psychiatric Bulletin*, **15**, 26–27.

Jones, L. & Lodge, A. (1991). A survey of psychiatric patients: Views of outpatient clinic facilities. *Health Bulletin*, **49**, 320–328.

Jones, L., Lenerman, L.P. & Maclean, U. (1987). *Consumer Feedback for the NHS: A Literature Review*. London: Kings Fund College.

Jones, P. (1992). Patients' perception of health as a measure of outcome. *Medical Audit News*, **2**(4), 57–58.

Kat, B. (1993). Psychology in health care: Death and rebirth. *Psychologist*, **6**, 123–125.

Kerrison, S., Packwood, T. & Buxton, M. (1993). *Medical Audit: Taking Stock*. London: Kings Fund Centre.

Kerrison, S., Packwood, K. & Buxton, M. (1994). Monitoring medical audit. In Robinson R. & Le Grand, J. (eds), *Evaluating the NHS Referral*. London: Kings Fund Institute.

Kingdon, D. (1994). Care programme approach: Recent government policy and legislation. *Psychiatric Bulletin*, **18**, 68–70.

Klein, R. (1995). *The New Politics of the NHS* (3rd edn). London: Longman.

Knapp, M., Beecham, J., Koutsogeorgopoulou, V., Hallam, A., Fenyo, A., Marks, I.M., Connolly, J., Audini, B. & Muijen, M. (1994). Service use and costs of home-based versus hospital-based care for people with serious mental illness. *British Journal of Psychiatry*, **165**, 195–203.

Knight, S. (1995). The NHS information management and technology strategy from a mental health perspective. *Advances in Psychiatric Treatment*, **1**, 223–229.

Koch, H.C.H. (1991). *Exceeding Expectations: Total Quality Management in Mental Health Services*. Hove: Pavilion Publishing.

Kotter, J.P. & Schlesinger, L.A. (1979). Choosing strategies for change. In Mayon-White, B. (ed.), *Planning and Managing change*. London: Harper & Row.

Krowinski, W. & Fitt, D. (1978). A model for evaluating mental health programmes. *Administration & Mental Health*, **6**(1), 22–41.

Larsen, D.L., Attkisson, C.C., Hargreaves, W.A. & Nguyen, T.D. (1979). Assessment of client/patient satisfaction: Development of a general scale. *Evaluation and Programme Planning*, **2**, 197–207.

Lavender, A., Leiper, R., Pilling, S. & Clifford, P. (1994). Quality assurance in mental health: the QUARTZ system. *British Journal of Clinical Psychology*, **33**, 451–467.

Leahy, A. & Winkley, L. (1992). Multidisciplinary audit in child and adolescent psychiatry. *Psychiatric Bulletin*, **16**, 214–215.

LeBow, J. (1982). Consumer satisfaction with mental health treatment. *Psychological Bulletin*, **91**(2), 244–259.

Lefanu, J. (ed.) (1994). *Preventionitis: The Exaggerated Claims of Health Promotion*. London: Social Affairs Unit.

Lelliott, P. (1994a). An update on the activities of the College Research Unit. *Psychiatric Bulletin*, **18**, 58–60.

Lelliott, P. (1994b). Making clinical informatics work. *British Medical Journal*, **308**, 802–803.

Lelliott, P. (1994c). Local audit of suicide. In Jenkins, R., Griffiths, S., Wiley, I., Hawton, K., Morgan, G. & Tylee, A. (eds), *The Prevention of Suicide*. London: HMSO.

Lelliott, P. (1995a). *A Monitoring Tool for the Care Programme Approach*. London: Royal College of Psychiatrists Research Unit, March.

Lelliott, P. (1995b). Mental health information systems and minimal data sets. In Wing, J.K. (ed.), *Measurement for Mental Health: Contributions from the College Research Unit*. Research Unit Publications (RUP) 2. London: Royal College of Psychiatrists, 89–101.

Lelliott, P. (1995c). Mental health information systems: Problems and opportunities. *Advances in Psychiatric Treatment*, **1**, 216–222.

Lelliott, P. & Strathdee, G. (1992). The one-day census in clinical audit. *Psychiatric Bulletin*, **16**, 614–615.

Lelliott, P. & Wing, J.K. (1994). A national audit of new long-stay psychiatric patients. II. Impact on services. *British Journal of Psychiatry*, **165**, 170–178.

Lelliott, P., Flannagan, C. & Shanks, S. (1993). *A Review of Seven Mental Health Information Systems: A Functional Perspective*. London: Royal College of Psychiatrists.

Lelliott, P., Wing, J.K. & Clifford, P. (1994). A national audit of new long-stay psychiatric patients. I. Method and description of the cohort. *British Journal of Psychiatry*, **165**, 160–169.

Lethem, R. (1995). Aftercare: Who attends Section 117 meetings? *Psychiatric Bulletin*, **19**, 106–107.

Ley, P. & Morris, L.A. (1984). Psychological aspects of written information for patients. In S. Rachman (ed.), *Contributions to Medical Psychology*, Vol. 3. Oxford: Pergamon.

Lippitt, R. & White, R.K. (1952). An experimental study of leadership. In Swanson, G.E., Newcomb, T.M. & Hartley, E.L. (eds), *Readings in Social Psychology*. London: Holt.

Lippitt, R., Watson, J. & Westley, B. (1958). *The Dynamics of Planned Change*. New York: Harcourt, Brace & World.

Littlejohn, P. (1996). Using contracts to develop clinical audit. Paper given at the Second National Conference on Audit in Mental Health Services. Royal College of Psychiatrists/Community Health Sheffield NHS Trust, Sheffield.

Lovell, K., Marks, I., Noshirvani, H. & O'Sullivan, G. (1994). Should treatment distinguish anxiogenic from anxiolytic obsessive-compulsive ruminations? Results of a pilot controlled study and of a clinical audit. *Psychotherapy and Psychosomatics*, **61**, 150–155.

Lyons, C. & Gumbert, R. (1990). Medical audit data: Counting is not enough. *British Medical Journal*, **300**, 563–566.

Mai, F., Gosselin, J., Varan, L., Bourgon, L. et al (1993). Effects of treatment and alternative care on length of stay on a general hospital psychiatric unit: Results of an audit. *Canadian Journal of Psychiatry*, **38**, 39–45.

Malan, D.H. (1976). *The Frontier of Brief Psychotherapy*. New York: Plenum.

Mallett, J. (1991). Shifting the focus of audit. *Health Service Journal*, February, 24–25.

Marinker, M. (1990). *Medical Audit and General Practice*. London: British Medical Journal.

Marks, F.M. (1977). The characteristics of psychiatric patients readmitted within a month of discharge. *Psychological Medicine*, **7**, 345–352.

Marks, I.M., Connolly, J., Muijen, M., Audini, B., McNamee, G. & Lawrence, R.E. (1994). Home-based versus hospital-based care for people with serious mental illness. *British Journal of Psychiatry*, **165**, 179–194.

Marriott, S. & Cape, J. (1995). Clinical practice guidelines for clinical psychologists. *Clinical Psychology Forum*, **81**, 2–6.

Marriott, S. & Lelliott, P. (1994). *Clinical Practice Guidelines and their developments*. London: Royal College of Psychiatrists Counsel reports CR34, June.

Matthews, B. (1995). Introducing the care programme approach to a multi-disciplinary team: The impact on clinical practice. *Psychiatric Bulletin*, **19**, 143–145.

Maxwell, R.J. (1984). Quality assessment in health. *British Medical Journal*, **288**, 1470–1472.

Maynard, A. (1993). Auditing medical audit. *Medical Audit News*, **3**(5), 67–68.

McAuliffe, E. & MacLachlan, M. (1992). Consumers' views of mental health services: The good, the bad and some suggestions for improvements. *Clinical Psychology Forum*, **47**, 16–19.

McCarthy, A., Roy, D., Holloway, F., Attican, S. & Goss, T. (1995). Supervision registers and the care programme approach; A practical solution. *Psychiatric Bulletin*, **19**, 195–199.

McClelland, R. (1995). Editorial: Health informatics. *Advances in Psychiatric Treatments*, **1**, 214–215.

McKee, M. (1993). Routine data: A resource for clinical audit. *Quality in Health Care*, **2**(2), 104–111.

McPherson, K. (1989). Why do variations occur? in Anderson, T. & Mooney, G. (eds), *The Challenge of Medical Practice Variations*. London: Macmillan.

Millington, C. & Slator, W. (1995). *Care Programme Approach in Action: The Derbyshire Experience*. Community Health Care Service (North Derbyshire) NHS Trust.

Mitchell, F. & Fowkes, M. (1985). Audit reviewed: Does feedback of performance change clinical behaviour? *Journal of Royal College of Physicians*, **19**, 251–254.

Mockler, D.M. & Riordan, J.M. (1992). *Care Planning and Clinical Audit*. Paper presented at the "Partnership in Audit" conference, York, November.

Morgan, H. (1994). *Clinical Audit of Suicide and Other Unexpected Deaths*. (NHSE: HSG(94)21). Leeds: Department of Health.

Morgan, H. & Owen, J. (1990). *Persons at Risk of Suicide: Guidelines on Good Clinical Practice*. Nottingham: Boots.

Morgan, H. & Priest, P. (1991). Suicide and other unexpected deaths among psychiatric in-patients. The Bristol confidential enquiry. *British Journal of Psychiatry*, **158**, 368–374.

Morrison, L. (1991). Evaluation of an information pamphlet describing psychological work with people who have chronic pain. *Clinical Psychology Forum*, **34**, 29–31.

Moseley, T. (1996). Planning clinical audit and implementing change. Paper given at the Second National Conference on Audit in Mental Health Services. Royal College of Psychiatrists/Community Health Sheffield NHS Trust, Sheffield.

Myers, B.A. (1969). *A Guide to Medical Care Administration: Concepts and Principles.* Washington DC: American Public Health Association.

Nadler, D.A. (1993). Concepts for the management of organisational change. In Mabey, C. & Mayon-White, B. (eds), *Managing Change* (2nd edn). Milton Keynes: Open University.

Naik, P. & Lee, A. (1994). Processing and assessing psychiatric referrals. *Psychiatric Bulletin,* **18,** 480–482.

National Audit Office (1994). *Auditing Clinical Care in Scotland.* London: HMSO.

National Audit Office (1995). *Clinical Audit in England.* London: HMSO.

Newnes, C. (1988). A note on waiting lists. *Clinical Psychology Forum,* **13,** 15–18.

NHSE (1994a). *Reports on the Medical, Primary Care and Royal College Audit Programmes 1989–1994.* Leeds: Department of Health.

NHSE (1994b). *Report on the Nursing and Therapy Audit Programme 1991–1994.* Leeds: Department of Health.

NHSE (1994c). *Improving the Effectiveness of the NHS.* EL(1994) 74. Leeds: Department of Health.

NHSE (1995a). *Improving the effectiveness of clinical services.* EL(95)105. Leeds.

NHSE (1995b). *The New Health Authorities and the Clinical Audit Initiative: Outline of Planned Monitoring Arrangements.* EL(1995)103. Leeds: Department of Health.

NHSE (1996a). *CPA: Taking Stock and Moving On.* Leeds: NHSE.

NHSE (1996b). *Terms, Records, and Information: An Introduction to Using Computerised Information and the Read Coded Clinical Terms in Nursing, Midwifery and Health Visiting Practice.* Loughborough: NHS CCC.

NHSME (1993a). *Meeting and Improving Standards in Healthcare: A Quality Statement on the Development of Clinical Audit.* EL(1993)59. London: Department of Health.

NHSME (1993b). *Improving Clinical Effectiveness.* EL(1993)115. London: Department of Health.

NHSME (1994). *Clinical Audit: 1994/95 and Beyond.* EL(94)20. Leeds: Department of Health.

Nunnally, J.C. (1978). *Psychometric Theory* (2nd edn). New York: McGraw-Hill.

Oakland, J.S. (1989). *Total Quality Management.* Oxford: Heinemann.

OECD (1987). *Financing and Delivering Health Care.* Paris: OECD.

OECD (1995). *Internal Markets in the Making of Health Systems in Canada, Iceland and the UK.* Health Policy studies Number 6. Paris: OECD.

Olsen, R. (1992). Measuring effectiveness in psychiatric care. In Green, S. (ed.), *Measuring Outcomes in the Mental Health Service.* HSMC, University of Birmingham.

Orrell, M.W. & Johnson, S. (1992). Three psychiatric day centres in a London borough. *Psychiatric Bulletin,* **16,** 540–542.

Ovretveit, J. (1991). *Quality Health Services,* Uxbridge: BIOSS, Brunel University.

Ovretveit, J. (1992). *Health Services Quality.* London, Blackwell Scientific Publications.

Owers, D. (1996). *Is Psychiatry Amenable to Clinical Audit.* Paper presented at Clinical Audit in Psychiatry Conference, Royal College of Psychiatrists Research Unit, London, April.

Packwood, T. & Kober, A. (1995). *Making use of Clinical Audit: A Guide to Practice in the Health Professions.* Buckingham, OU Press.

Parry, G. (1992). Improving psychotherapy services: Applications of research, audit and evaluation. *British Journal of Clinical Psychology,* **31,** 3–19.

Parry, G. & Watts, F. (1982). *Behavioural and Mental Health Research: A Handbook of Skills and Methods.* Hove: Erlbaum.

Patten, P. (1991). Psychiatric Audit. *Psychiatric Bulletin,* **15**, 550–551.

Paxton, R. (1995). Audit and research: Mutually supportive. *Clinical Psychology Forum,* **86**, 8–11.

Perkins, B. & Fisher, N. (1996). Beyond mere existence: The auditing of care plans. *Journal of Mental Health,* **5**(3), 275–286.

Peters, T. (1987). *Thriving on Chaos: Handbook for a Management Revolution.* New York: Alfred A. Knopf.

Pfeffer, N. (1992). Strings attached. *Health Service Journal,* **102**, 22–23.

Pincus, H. (1996). *The US Experience of Audit.* Paper given at Royal College of Psychiatry Conference: Clinical Audit in Psychiatry, Royal Society of Medicine, London, April.

Pippard, J. (1992a). Auditing the administration of ECT. *Psychiatric Bulletin,* **16**, 59–62.

Pippard, J. (1992b). Audit of electroconvulsive treatment in two National Health Service regions. *British Journal of Psychiatry,* **160**, 621–637.

Pippard, J. & Ellam, L. (1981). Electroconvulsive treatment in Great Britain. *British Journal of Psychiatry,* **139**, 563–568.

Rands, E. (1992). Who does what for whom? Audit and dynamics of an acute psychogeriatric assessment unit. *International Journal of Geriatric Psychiatry,* **7**, 291–296.

Reddy, S. & Pitt, B. (1993). What becomes of demented patients referred to a psychogeriatric unit? An approach to audit. *International Journal of Geriatric Psychiatry,* **8**, 175–180.

Reiman, S. (1989). Multi-disciplinary teamwork in a community setting: A discussion paper. *Clinical Psychology Forum,* **19**, 18–21.

Riches, T., Steak, L. & Espie, C. (1994). Introducing anticipated recovery pathways: A teaching hospital experience. *Health Care Quality Assurance,* **7**(5), 21–28.

Rigge, M. (1994). Involving patients in clinical audit. *Quality in Health Care* (Suppl.), **3**, S2–S5.

Riordan, J.M. & Mockler, D.M. (1994). *Care Programme Evaluation and Concurrent Audit in Psychiatry.* Presented at "Improving Care Through Clinical Audit" Conference, Department of Health, Birmingham NEC, February.

Riordan, J.M. & Mockler, D.M. (1996). Audit of care programming in an acute psychiatric admission ward for the elderly. *International Journal of Geriatric Psychiatry,* **11**, 109–118.

Ritchie, J., Dick, D. & Langham, R. (1994). *The Report of the Enquiry into the Care and Treatment of Christopher Clounis.* London: HMSO.

Rix, S., Christie, M. & Wing, J.K. (1993). The role of the mental health SWG in the development of the Read codes. *Clinical Psychology Forum.* **62**, 34–36.

Robertson, C., Wheeldon, T., Eagles, J.M. & Reid, I.C. (1995). Improving electroconvulsive therapy practice through audit. *Psychiatric Bulletin,* **19**, 480–481.

Robinson, M. (1991). Medical audit: Basic principles and current methods. *Psychiatric Bulletin,* **15**, 21–23.

Robinson, R. & Le Grand, J. (eds) (1994). *Evaluating the NHS Reforms.* London: Kings Fund Centre.

Robson, M. (1982). *Quality Circles: A practical guide.* London: Gower.

Rodwin, M. (1995). Conflicts in managed care. *New England Journal of Medicine,* **332**, 604–607.

Ross-Davies, A. (1994). Patient defined outcomes. *Quality in Health Care* (Suppl.), **3**, S6–S9.

Rossiter, J. (1991). Suicide. *Psychiatric Bulletin*, **15**, 674–675.

Roth, A.D. & Fonagy, P. (1996). *What Works For Whom?: A Critical Review of Psychotherapy Research*. New York: Guilford Press.

Roy, D. (1991). Setting up district audit meetings in psychiatry. *Psychiatric Bulletin*, **15**, 417–418.

Royal College of Psychiatrists (1992). *Facilities and Services for Patients who have Chronic Persisting Severe Disabilities Resulting from Mental Illness*. Council Report CR19. London: RCP.

Royal College of Physicians of London (1989). *Medical Audit: A First Report*. London: Royal College of Physicians.

Royal College of Physicians of London (1993). *Medical Audit: A Second Report*. London: Royal College of Physicians.

Rumsey, M., Walshe, K., Bennett, J. & Coles, J. (1993). *Evaluating Medical Audit. The Role of the Commissioner in Audit: Findings of a National Survey of Commissioning Authorities in England*. London: CASPE.

Rusius, C. (1992). The Mental Health Act 1983: What does the Patient Think? *Psychiatric Bulletin*, **16**, 268–269.

Russell, I.T. & Wilson, B.J. (1992). Audit: The third clinical science. *Quality in Health Care*, **1**(1), 51.

Rutter, M. (1982). Psychological therapies in child psychiatry: Issues and prospects. *Psychological Medicine*, **12**, 723–740.

Ryle, A. (1990). *Cognitive-Analytic Therapy: Active participation in change?* Chichester: Wiley.

Salancik, G.R. & Pfeffer, J. (1977). Who gets power and how they hold onto it: A strategic-contingency model of power. *Organizational Dynamics*, Winter, 3–21.

Scheffe, H.A. (1953). A method for judging all possible contrasts in the analysis of variance. *Biometrika*, **40**, 87–104.

Scheffe, H.A. (1959). *The Analysis of Variance*. New York: Wiley.

Schein, E.J. (1988). *Process Consultation: Its role in Organizational Development*. Reading, MA: Addison-Wesley.

Schreter, B. (1993). Ten trends in managed care and their impact on the biopsychosocial model. *Hospital and Community Psychiatry*, **44**, 325–327.

Scottish Home and Health Department (1990). *Code of Practice*. Edinburgh: HMSO.

Seager, M. & Jacobson, R. (1991). Tackling waiting lists: Beyond a quantitative perspective. *Clinical Psychology Forum*, **35**, 29–32.

Shah A. & Ames, D. (1994). in the *International Review of Psychiatry* (abstract rev.)

Shaw, C.D. (1986). *Introducing Quality Assurance*, London: Kings Fund paper no. 64.

Shaw, C. (1989). *Medical Audit: Hospital Handbook*. London: Kingston Centre.

Shaw, C. (1996). *What has Audit Achieved so Far?* Paper given at Clinical Audit in Psychiatry Conference: Royal College of Psychiatrists Research Unit, London.

Shawe-Taylor, M., Richards, J., Sage, N. & Young, E. (1994). Assessment appointments prior to being placed on the waiting list. *Clinical Psychology Forum*, **70**, 23–25.

Shepherd, G., King, C., Tillbury, J. & Fowler, D. (1995). Implementing the care programme approach. *Journal of Mental Health*, **4**, 261–274.

Simpson, L. & Brown, J. (1993). Patient protocols. *Health Care Quality Assurance*, **6**(6), 10–16.

Slade, M. (1996). Measuring clinical outcomes: A response to Barkham and colleagues. *Clinical Psychology Forum*, **90**, 25–26.

Smith, C. (1993). Was it because of what we did that things changed. *Medical Audit News*, **3**(10), 158.

Solihull Health Authority (1992). *A Report on Collaborative Care Planning*. SHA.

Song, H., Freemantle, N., Sheldon, T., House, A., Watson, P., Long, A. & Mason, J. (1993). Selective serotonin reuptake inhibitors: Meta-analysis of efficacy and acceptability. *British Medical Journal*, **306**, 683–687.

Spear, J., Cole, A. & Scott, J. (1995). A cross-sectional evaluation of a community-orientated mental health service. *Psychiatric Bulletin*, **19**, 151–154.

Spielberger, C.D., Gorsuch, R.L., Lushene, R., Vagg, P.R. & Jacobs, G.A. (1983). *Manual for State–Trait Anxiety Inventory*. Palo Alto, CA: Consulting Psychologists Press.

Stallard, P. (1996). Validity and reliability of the Parent Satisfaction Questionnaire. *British Journal of Clinical Psychology*, **35**, 311–318.

Stallard, P. & Chadwick, R. (1991). Consumer evaluation: A cautionary note. *Clinical Psychology Forum*, **34**, 2–4.

Startup, M. (1994). Dealing with waiting lists for adult mental health services. *Clinical Psychology Forum*, **68**, 5–9.

Steering Committee CIHS (1995). *Report of a Confidential Enquiry into Homicides and Suicides by Mentally Ill People*. London: Royal College of Psychiatrists.

Stiles, W., Putnam, S., Wolf, M. & James, S. (1979). Interaction exchange structure and patient satisfaction with medical interviews. *Medical Care*, **17**, 667–681.

Stott, R. (1993). Clinical rather than medical audit. *Medical Audit News*, **3**(5), 70–72.

Swinehart, K. & Green, R. (1995). Continuous improvement and TQM in health care: An emerging operational paradigm becomes a strategic imperative. *Health Care Quality Assurance*, **8**(1), 23–27.

Tantum, D., Goter, R., Jackson, G., Amall, S., Fitzgerald, J., Perceval, C., Purlackee, R. & Stratton, M. (1992). Auditing the community team. *Journal of Mental Health*, **1**, 327–334.

Taylor, J. & Dewar, I. (1994). Lithium audit in the Scottish borders. *Psychiatric Bulletin*, **18**, 620–621.

Thomas, L.H., McColl, E., Priest, J., Bond, S. & Boys, R.J. (1996). Newcastle satisfaction with nursing scales: An instrument for quality assessment of nursing care. *Quality in Health Care*, **5**(2), 67–72.

Thompson, C. (1994). The use of high-dose antipsychotic medication. *British Journal of Psychiatry*, **164**, 448–458.

Thomson, R. & Barton, A. (1994). Is audit running out of steam? *Quality in Health Care*, **3**, 225–229.

Thomson, R., Cook, G., Lelliott, P., Baker, I. & Godwin, R. (1993). *Audit and the Purchaser/Provider Interaction* (EL, 93)34. London: Department of Health.

Thomson, R., Elcoat, C. & Pugh, E. (1996). Clinical audit and the purchaser/provider interaction: Different attitudes and expectations in the United Kingdom. *Quality in Health Care*, **5**, 97–103.

Treadwell, T., Howell, H. & Bramley, J. (1995). *People and the Care Programme Approach*. Southern Derbyshire Mental Health Trust.

Tukey, J.W. (1949). One degree of freedom for additivity. *Biometrics*, **5**, 232–242.

Tukey, J.W. (1953). *The Problem of Multiple Comparisons*. Unpublished manuscript, Princeton University.

Tukey, J.W. (1977). *Exploratory Data Analysis*. Reading, MA: Addison-Wesley.

Tushman, M.L. (1977). A political approach to organisations: A review and rationale. *Academy of Management Review*, **2**, 206–216.

Tyrer, P. & Owen, R. (1984). Anxiety in primary care: Is short-term drug treatment appropriate? *Journal of Psychiatric Research*, **18**, 73–79.

Victor, C. & Vetter, N. (1989). Measuring outcome after discharge from hospital for the elderly: A conceptual and empirical investigation. *Archives of Gerontology and Geriatrics*, **8**, 87–94.

Vroom, V.H. (1964). *Work and Motivation*. New York: Wiley.

Vroom, V.H. & Yetton, P.W. (1973). *Leadership and Decision Making*. Pittsburgh: University of Pittsburgh Press.

Vuori, H.V. (1982). *Quality Assurance of Health Services: Concepts and Methodologies* (16th edn). Geneva: World Health Organization.

Walshe, K. (1994). *The impact of Medical Audit*. Keynote Address at the "Cutting Edge of Practice" Conference, Sheffield, November.

Walshe, K. & Coles, J. (1993). Evaluating audit: A review of initiatives. London: CASPE.

Ward, P. (1994). The mental health market: Recent Government policy on legislation. *Psychiatric Bulletin*, **18**, 538–540.

Ware, J.E. & Sherbourne, C.D. (1992). The MOS 36 item short-form health survey (SF-36): Conceptual framework and item selection. *Medical Care*, **30**, 473–483.

Ware, J.E., Snyder, M.K., Wright, W. & Davies, A.R. (1983). Defining and measuring patient satisfaction with medical care. *Evaluation and Program Planning*, **6**, 247–263.

Warner, J.P., Singhal, S. & Dutta, A. (1994). How well do we assess patient satisfaction? *Medical Audit News*, **4**, 157–158.

Warner, P., Slade, R. & Barnes, T. (1995). Change in neuroleptic prescribing practice. *Psychiatric Bulletin*, **19**, 237–239.

Webb, M.D. & Harvey, I.M. (1994). Auditing the introduction of audit. *Medical Audit News*, **4**(2), 19–20.

Weiner, J. (1994). *Quality Assurance and Assessment and Emerging Health Care Reform in Mental Health Systems*. Paper given at "The Cutting Edge of Practice": National Conference on Audit in Mental Health Services: Cutler's Hall, Sheffield, November.

Weinstein, R.M. (1979). Patient attitudes towards mental hospitalisation: A review of quantitative research. *Journal of Health and Social Behaviour*, **20**, 237–258.

Welsh, S. (1994). NHS trusts: Recent government policy and legislation. *Psychiatric Bulletin*, **18**, 131–134.

Wesson, M. & Rigby, J. (1994). Improved conformity with Mental Health Act. *Medical Audit News*, **4**(10), 150–152.

White, J. (1992). How to get round the waiting list? Using the local press and public lectures to publicise stress. *Clinical Psychology Forum*, **42**, 6–9.

White, C. (1995). Care plans by code. *Advances in Psychiatric Treatment*, **1**, 230–236.

Williams, A. (1988). Health economics: The end of clinical freedom. *British Medical Journal*, **297**, 1183–1186.

Willmot, M., Foster, J., Walsh, K. & Coulds, J. (1995). *Evaluating Audit: A Review of Audit Activity in the Nursing and Therapy Professions*. Findings of a national survey. London: CASPE.

Wing, J. (1992). *Epidemiologically Based Mental Health Needs Assessments*. London: Royal College of Psychiatrists.

Wing, J.K. (1993). Read codes for the mental health professions. The Clinical Terms Project. *Psychiatric Bulletin*, **17**, 195–196.

Wing, J.K. (1994). Measuring mental health outcomes: A perspective from the Royal College of Psychiatrists. In Delamothe T. (ed.), *Outcomes into Clinical Practice*. London: BMA, 147–152.

Wing, J. (1996) *Measuring Outcomes in Psychiatry*. Paper given at Clinical Audit in Psychiatry Conference, Royal College of Psychiatrists Research Unit, London.

Wing, J.K. & Rix, S.R. (1994). Read codes for the mental health professions: An update. *Psychiatric Bulletin*, **18**, 234–235.

Wing, J., Curtis, R. & Beevor, A. (1994). Health of the Nation: Measuring mental health outcomes. *Psychiatric Bulletin*, **18**, 690–691.

Wing, J., Rix, S. & Curtis, R. (1995). *Schizophrenia (Vol. 2): Protocol for Assessing Services for People with Severe Mental Illness*. Developed for Clinical Standards Advisory Group (CSAG). London: HMSO.

Wishert, J., Knight, S. & Gehlhaar, E. (1993). Deliberate self-harm: An audit of a service to patients. *Health Care Quality Assurance*, **6**(2), 4–9.

Wyke, T. (1995). *Ever Slimmer Health Care: The World in 1996*. London: The Economist Publications, 114.

Yassin, T. & Watkins, S. (1993). What influences care planning? Nurses attitudes towards care plans. *Professional Nurse*, **8**, 572–577.

Yates, F. (1934). Contingency tables involving small numbers and the chi squared test. Supplement. *Journal of the Royal Statistical Society (Series B)*, **1**, 217–235.

Yesavage, M. & Brink, T. (1983). Development and validation of a geriatric depression scale: A preliminary report. *Journal of Psychiatric Research*, **17**(1), 37–49.

Yesavage, J.A., Brink, T.L., Rose, T.L., Lum, O., Huang, V., Adey, M.B. & Leirer, V.O. (1983). Development and validation of a geriatric depression scale: A preliminary report. *Journal of Psychiatric Research*, **17**, 37–49.

Yesavage, J.A., Brink, T.L. Rose, T.L. & Adey, M. (1986). The geriatric depression rating scale: Comparison with other self report and psychiatric rating scales. In L. Poon (ed.), *Handbook for Clinical Memory Assessment of Older Adults*. Washington, DC: American Psychological Association, 153–167.

Zarin, D., Pincus, H. & McIntyre, J. (1993). Practice Guidelines. *American Journal of Psychiatry*, **150**, 175–177.

Zigmond, A.S. & Snaith, R.P. (1983). The Hospital Anxiety and Depression Scale. *Acta Psychiatrica Scandinavia*, **67**, 361–370.

APPENDIX 1

CASE STUDY EXAMPLE: MR H

Mr H is a 75-year-old man with a previous (five-year) history of psychotic illness, living on his own, admitted on Section 2 because of severe personal neglect, not eating, not changing his clothes, not washing, living in squalor and because of the neighbours' concerns regarding the condition of his two Alsatian dogs. Mr H had been relocated to his current flat six weeks previously from a neighbouring borough following eviction from his previous abode due to its being condemned. His case had been taken up by the local Social Work Department but in the intervening period he was defaulting on his medication, and was refusing entry to the Community Psychiatric Nursing Service for depot injection and Social Services Home Care and Domiciliary Support. Early impressions noted by the named nurse include quite severe agitation in being placed in hospital, isolating himself from the ward, reluctance to engage in any social discourse, mistrustful and uncommunicative.

First-Post-assessment Ward Review Discussion

Ward doctor gives brief history leading to Mr H's admission to hospital. The ward manager indicated that Mr H had appeared quite paranoid, expressing the idea that someone is going to cut his throat on the ward. The ward doctor decided to increase haloperidol to 2.5 mg b.d. The ward manager also indicated that Mr H seemed to show signs of depression, isolating himself, showing loss of appetite and withdrawn behaviour. The ward doctor decided to put Mr H on sertraline medication 100 mg daily. The team discussed the fact that Mr H when at home was defaulting on his medication and possible ways of ensuring Mr H takes his medication on return to his home. A possible introduction of a depot injection to replace the haloperidol was considered. This would be administered by the CPN, and was agreed by the CPN. A test dose of depot neuroleptic medication would be given to the patient, 10 mg Depixol. Once Mr H was commenced on the depot injection and the acute part of his illness had settled, gradual reduction of the haloperidol medication would commence, leaving Mr H taking the depot injection. It was thought that an occupational therapy assessment would be required fairly soon; the ward doctor stated that he would send a referral requesting assessment – referral to be completed by 10 June 1993. With regard to Mr H's home situation, the social worker stated that a full home assessment and assessment of future domiciliary care support needs would have to be completed. This assessment was due to be completed prior to admission and before his resulting breakdown. The

CARE PLAN

Name . . . .   CPA/IPC 3.A.

PROBLEMS /NEEDS	SPECIFIC AIMS/ GOALS	TEAM PLAN/INTERVENTIONS	PERSON RESPONSIBLE	REVIEW DATE

Patient/Carer's Signature _____ Date _____ Named Nurse/Key worker's Signature _____ Date _____

Patient's Comments:

MULTI-DISCIPLINARY REVIEW

NAME: _____

Present:

Problem No.	PREVIOUS INTERVENTIONS	Problem Res.*	NEW PROBLEM / INTERVENTION IDENTIFIED (Transfer to Care Plan)

DECISIONS/ACTIONS:

NEXT REVIEW DATE: ..... / ..... / ..... Signed .... Designation .... Date:

Copy (where applicable) to: Client ....   CPA Secretary, Psychology Dept ....   Medical file ....   CMHT file ....   GP ......   Other ....

* PROBLEM RESOLUTION SCALE   1 = Unresolved   2 = Partially Resolved   3 = Resolved

HoNOS Rate 9 if not known or not applicable

1 Aggression	2 Self harm	3 Alcohol, drugs	4 Memory, orientation	5 Physical problems	6 Mood disturbance
7 Hallucinations, delusions	8 Other mental/behavioural probs	9 Social relationships	10 Housing/locality	11 Employment, recreation, finance	12 Functional disability (scale 0–100)

assessment was not completed due to changes in social services structure, resulting in delayed allocation of the social worker. The social worker had made contact with the RSPCA kennels for temporary holding of Mr H's two Alsatian dogs. The social worker is to meet with Mr H on 11 June 1993 at 10 a.m. to discuss the possibility of taking his two dogs into permanent care and the possible adoption scheme conducted by the RSPCA as it seems to be the case that Mr H was unable to care for his two dogs at home. This would naturally have a great impact on Mr H as he has grown quite attached to his two dogs. The social worker has agreed to see Mr H on a weekly basis for three quarters of an hour on a Wednesday from 10 a.m. to 10.45 a.m. over a four-week period to discuss his home problems and the present problems with his dogs. The occupational therapist had completed an occupational therapy assessment to identify what possible ward-based activities Mr H would benefit from participating in. The report was due to be submitted yesterday for discussion in the review, but the occupational therapist was unable to document her assessment and attend the review to give the report. The named nurse had contacted the occupational therapist and she stated she would send the report before next week's review. The named nurse had indicated that Mr H was continuing not to eat and seemed to be suffering from weight loss. It was decided in the review that a daily weight check should be completed and that the nursing staff should monitor Mr H's dietary intake. The night nurse had also indicated that Mr H was restless through the night, sleeping for only one or two hours. It was also decided that a sleep chart should be kept to monitor Mr H's sleeping pattern. Mr H had indicated to the named nurse that he was not happy with the move from his previous house to the relocation in the Borough. This apparently seemed to be the antecedent for Mr H's breakdown. The social worker indicated that they would look into the housing situation and contact the Housing Department by letter. The letter would go off by 14 June 1993. The named nurse agreed to complete a personal care assessment and to feedback to the review by the next meeting on 15 June 1993. It was felt by the team that Mr H on returning home would require more extensive domiciliary care, although social services could not currently provide this sort of intense package due to insufficient resources.

CARE PLAN

Name: Mr H

	PROBLEMS/NEEDS	OUTCOME GOALS		PLAN	TARGET DATE	SERVICE CODE
1.	Neglect of self and personal hygiene	Establish acceptable level of self care and personal hygiene	1. 2.	Personal care assessment Occupational therapy ward assessment programme identified	15.6.93 17.6.93	N OT
2.	Poor nutrition/not eating	Establish regular eating/provide adequate diet	1. 2.	Daily weight check Monitor dietary intake		N
3.	Recent arrival in unfamiliar area	Adopt and familiarise to new flat and locality	1.	Investigate reasons for recent move. Letter to Housing Department	14.6.93	SW
4.	No family or other support	Provide appropriate level of social support	1.	Social worker assessment for home care to be arranged	17.6.93	SW
5.	Squalid condition of flat	Clean flat: make ready for discharge	1. 2.	Occupational therapy home assessment Ward doctor to refer to occupational therapist	24.6.93 10.6.93	OT Dr
6.	Inability to care for dogs (Alsatians)	Arrange temporary care for dogs. Establish long-term care arrangements	1. 2. 3.	Social worker arrange RSPCA kennels Investigate long-term "adoption" Weekly session to discuss with patient (four weeks)	3.6.93 11.6.93 10.7.93	SW SW SW
7.	Previous history of schizophrenia	Investigate mental state/establish diagnosis. Provide treatment	1. 2.	Increase to haloperidol 25 mg b.d. Start setraline 100 mg		Dr/N Dr/N
8.	Mistrustful/isolated/ uncommunicative (paranoid)	Enable patient to indicate his needs	1.	Monitor effects of medication on mood and mental state		Dr/N
9.	Refusing medications/resisting services (Section 2)	Accept medication and helping services	1. 2.	Start Depixol (10 mg) test dose Administer and monitor depot injection on discharge		Dr/N CPN

APPENDIX 2: PROBLEM LIST

A	Physical	B	Psychological	C	Social
1	incontinence	1	hallucinated	1	lack of day activities
2	mobility	2	disordered speech	2	housing
3	restless/agitated	3	delusions	3	money
4	overactive	4	anxiety/fear	4	relationships
5	drug/alcohol abuse	5	depressed mood	5	social skills
6	dementia/memory loss	6	suicidality	6	isolation
7	appetite/weight loss	7	self-esteem	7	language
8	disturbed sleep pattern	8	aggression/hostility		
9	physical illness	9	depersonalisation		
10	self-neglect/self-care deficit	10	disorientated/confused		
11	side effects	11	dependence		
12	bingeing/vomiting	12	non-compliance		
13	overweight	13	defaulting on medication		
		14	grief/bereavement		
		15	mute		
		16	obsessional		
		17	hypochondria		
		18	phobic		
		19	sexual abuse		
		20	arson/fire risk		
		21	disinhibited		
		22	poor concentration		
		23	sexual identity		

APPENDIX 3: CASE STUDY EXAMPLE

A 69-year-old man was admitted with a past history of schizophrenia. The patient has always had learning difficulties.

Reason for admission (in brief):

Patient was found wandering the streets in a state of neglect. Lives alone experiencing auditory hallucinations, spending all his money on unknown items, not paying his bills. In receipt of Meals on Wheels service but patient rarely at home to receive his food. Patient is diagnosed as non-insulin-dependent diabetic. Only known community contact is the manager of local fish and chip shop.

	GDS	MMSE	GHQ	CR
Admission	8	21	16	4
Discharge	2	26	9	5

Geriatric Depression Scale:
   No evidence of depressive illness.

Mini Mental State Examination:
   Mild cognitive impairment on admission, in particular attention, recall and orientation. Five-point improvement on MMSE at discharge.

General Health Questionnaire:
   Some social anxiety and sleeping problems although minor on admission. Some improvement observed in these on discharge.

Crighton Royal
   Problems with communication, restlessness and dressing on admission. Post discharge, patient able to dress without prompting, but communication difficulties and restlessness still remained.

Presenting Problems

1. Experiencing auditory hallucinations: can hear neighbours through the walls plotting against him. Believes he is in danger in his flat.

2. Roams the streets and becomes incontinent.
3. Unable to manage finances. When purchasing items does not give correct money, allows shopkeeper to take amount and does not check his change. Community advice team contacted to arrange payment of bills by direct debit, and the rest of the money to be held in an account for spending money.
4. Diabetes, some doubt about diagnosis. Diagnosis confirmed, stable on medication.
5. Early-morning confusion.
6. Epilepsy.

Medication:
  Admission: Phenytoin
              Glibenclamide

  Discharge: Phenytoin 100 mg *mane*
              100 mg *nocte*
              Haloperidol 1 mg *mane*
              1 mg *nocte*
              Glibenclamide 5 mg *mane*

Length of stay:
  67 days

Discharged:
  Home: Meals on Wheels
  Juniper Day Hospital once weekly

Therapies in hospital:
  Chemotherapy

Assessments:
  Financial assessments
  Ability to self medicate
  Psychological assessment

Service Deficiencies

1. No community occupational therapist in post to complete home assessment and therefore no programmes in road safety, home care in his familiar environment able to be provided.
2. Difficulty in obtaining community assessments due to occupational therapy assistant requiring escort from qualified occupational therapist. Caused hold-up in completion of assessment.
3. Wait of two months for psychological assessment.
4. No suitable day care identifiable that would provide training and support in self-care and education programme to improve arithmetic abilities.
5. CATs could not provide direct debit from patients pension.
6. CAT members did not attend review meeting as agreed.

Client Satisfaction Questionnaire

1. Not involved in decision making and care planning of his care.
2. Had problems getting Meals on Wheels initially – stated it was urgent, took a few weeks to obtain.
3. Passed from service to service in health and social services, without any real purpose.
4. Information was adequate but could be improved.
5. Services gave what they could, but not really taking into consideration relatives problems.
6. Home care not easily obtained.
7. Did not agree with placement – brother had some reservations about patient's ability to care for himself.
8. Decisions made for relatives and patient as to what could be provided on discharge.

Problem Review at Two Months Follow-up

1. Financial difficulties still remain a problem (partially resolved).
2. Diabetes/epilepsy – stable on medication (resolved).
3. Confusion – remains, does not answer the door when people call and has locked himself out on a number of occasions, needing the police to let him in (unresolved).
4. Auditory hallucinations – remain a problem. Patient responding to hallucinations (unresolved).
5. Compliance with medication – some doubt as to whether patient is taking medication and, if he is, whether at appropriate times (partially resolved).

INDEX

Index compiled by Annette Musker